Dreamweaver®

8

Accelerated

Y.

Dreamweaver® 8 A c c e l e r a t e d

© 2006 Youngjin Singapore Pte, Ltd. World rights reserved.
Printed and bound in the Republic of Korea.

ISBN: 981-05-3848-0

How to contact us:

support@youngjin.com
feedback@youngjin.com.sg

Fax: 65-6339-1403

Credits

Author: H. M. Han
Manager: Suzie Lee
Production Editor: Patrick Cunningham
Editors: Elisabeth Beller, Bill Cassel
Book Designer: Litmus
Cover Designer: Chang-uk Lee
Indexer: S.H. Lee

Dreamweaver® 8

Accelerated

YJ IP Publishing Team

Installing Dreamweaver 8 > > >

This section provides information about installing and using Dreamweaver 8. Instructions for downloading and installing Adobe's 30-day trial version of Dreamweaver 8 are also included.

Downloading a Trial Version

If you do not have a copy of Dreamweaver 8, you can download a 30-day trial copy from the Adobe Web site.

[1] Start Internet Explorer. Type in http://www.Adobe.com in the address field and hit Enter. From the menu at the top of the Web page, choose Downloads > Trial downloads.

[2] Find Dreamweaver 8 in the product list and click on Try.

[3] In the Register and download window, type in your e-mail address and password (if you have one) and click Continue.

tip >>

If You Do Not Have a Password

If you don't have an Adobe password, select "No, I will create one now," and then click Continue. Type in the relevant information on the password setup page and then click Continue.

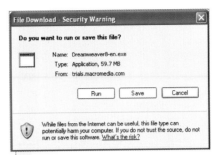

4 On the Adobe Trial Downloads page, you can download the trial program in the language and the operating system of your choice.

5 After making sure you meet the system requirements for Dreamweaver 8, click on Download. When the File Download dialog box appears, click Save.

6 In the Save As dialog box, choose the folder where you wish to save the trial program and then click Save.

7 Your download will begin automatically. Extract the file after downloading.

Installing Dreamweaver 8

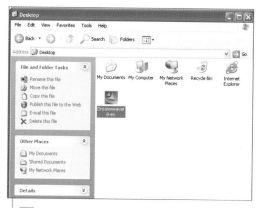

1 To start the installation, double-click the Dreamweaver 8 file.

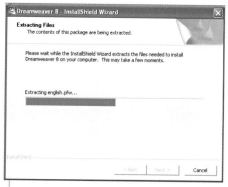

2 You should see the dialog box pictured here.

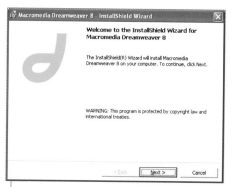

3 When you see the above dialog box, click Next to continue.

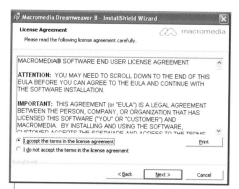

4 Before you can install the file, you will be asked to accept the license agreement. Click the Next button to accept the agreement and carry on with the installation. If you click Cancel, the installation will end.

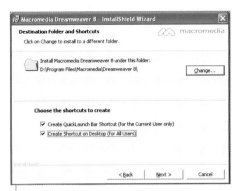

5 In this step, you will decide where to install the program. Click Next to install Dreamweaver in the Programs folder, or use the Change button to choose a different location.

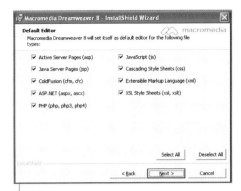

6 You will then be asked which file types you want to associate with Dreamweaver.

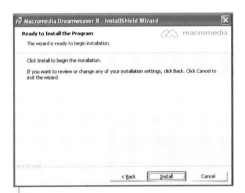

7 Click Install to begin installing or click Back to change your settings. You will need to go back to change the target drive if it does not have enough disk space.

8 When the installation has finished, you will see a message stating that the installation is complete. Click the Finish button to close the dialog box.

tip >>

Installing in Microsoft Windows 98 or 2000

When installing Dreamweaver 8 in Windows 98 or 2000, you will see a message that tells you to restart your computer after the installation is complete. Click Finish to end the installation and reboot your computer. You must reboot the computer in order for Dreamweaver to work properly.

Chapter 1

Getting Started with Dreamweaver 8

Web sites consist of HTML-based pages linked together in a systematic fashion. Writing complex code and organizing layouts can be done with a simple program such as Notepad (included with Windows), but it is not as easy as you might think. Macromedia Dreamweaver 8 allows you to produce complex layouts, advanced features, and visual elements in a simple, streamlined way. This chapter introduces Dreamweaver 8, including screen layouts, basic functions, and newly added features.

The Dreamweaver Concept and New Features

Dreamweaver is a WYSIWYG program, meaning that what you see as you create Web pages in Dreamweaver reflects what those pages will look like live on the Web. Beyond the simple entering of text, Dreamweaver allows you to design a layout with various objects (such as images, videos, and Flash files) using tables and layers. Moreover, it contains Web application features that can handle complex server scripts. To get things started, we'll explain the unique benefits of working in Dreamweaver, then describe some of the new features that have been added in version 8.

The Wonders of WYSIWYG

Even though HTML documents consist of simple elements, you need to write complex code according to HTML standards to create fully functional Web pages. Dreamweaver simplifies this process by allowing you to insert complex HTML tags and create Web pages as if drawing a picture.

The Dreamweaver start page

```
<html>
<head>
<title> </title>
</head>

<body>
</body>
</html>
```

Basic HTML format

Initially, Dreamweaver use was limited to general users and Web designers, but now that it has become a powerful tool with more advanced features, Web programmers can easily write server scripts to interact with databases. Furthermore, Dreamweaver 8 is designed to adapt to developments in Web technology, so taking the time to learn its use is a great way to future-proof your Web design skills.

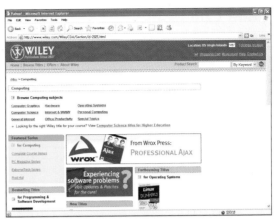

HTML tags

Web page

New Features of Dreamweaver 8

The Zoom and Hand Tools

Dreamweaver 8 has added Zoom and Hand tools like those found in most graphics programs to provide more convenience. The Zoom tool allows you to focus and zoom-in on specific areas of your page. The Hand tool allows you to easily move images to a desired position in the window.

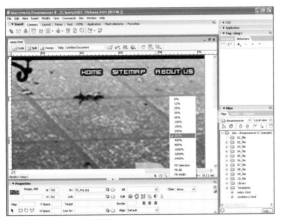

Viewing an image at 200%

Viewing an image at 50%

Code Collapsing, the Coding Toolbar, and the Snippets Panel

In Design view, you can create HTML documents with dozens of tables, images, and text blocks as if drawing a picture. Objects created in Design view are automatically transformed into HTML documents in Code view. However, most jobs are automatically processed, and sometimes code that you do not want will be created in the process. Furthermore, some problems generated from the creation and deletion of objects may not be solved in Design view. In such cases, you have to directly edit the HTML documents in Code view. You may find that the coding becomes very complex when many objects are inserted. Dreamweaver 8 offers a feature to easily simplify complex code, called code collapsing.

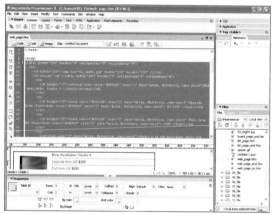

Standard HTML

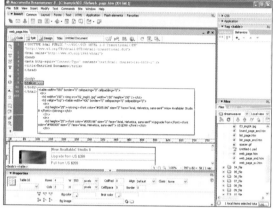

Collapsed code

The Coding toolbar, which allows you to easily add and apply various features in Code view, is a new feature that makes Dreamweaver more powerful.

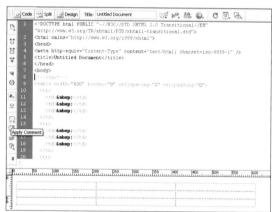

Coding toolbar

14

The Snippets panel allows you to save frequently used document forms or style and script sources that are not provided by Dreamweaver, which can be easily brought out from the Snippets panel later for use in other documents.

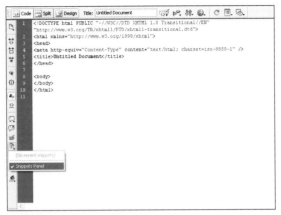

Snippets panel

Options for Work Window Management

Dreamweaver was originally a program for Web designers. However, it now provides the option to choose an interface familiar to Web programmers. The Coder, Designer, and Dual Screen layouts ensure that all user types are comfortable with the program.

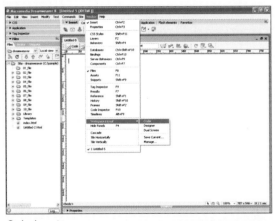

Coder layout

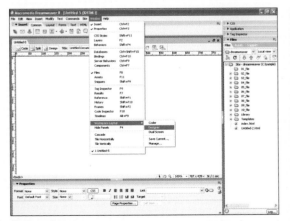

Designer layout

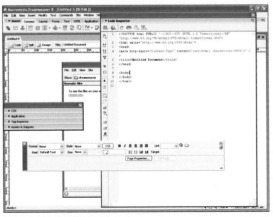

Dual Screen layout

15

Integrated CSS Panel

The new, integrated Cascading Style Sheet (CSS) panel allows you to create, edit, and manage all CSSs in one panel. For added convenience, you can also access CSS functionality from the Properties inspector, which allows you to create, edit, and select CSSs. For users of previous versions of Dreamweaver, the versatility of the new system will be a welcome improvement.

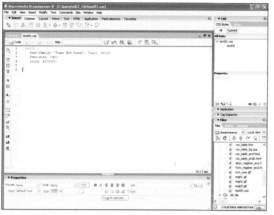

CSS panel

CSS dialog box

Drag-and-Drop XML Data

When you specify an XML file or the URL of a Web page, Dreamweaver allows you to drag-and-drop the corresponding fields to the page you are creating. You can also integrate XML-based data such as RSS (a protocol for Web syndication) with Web pages through a simple drag-and-drop workflow and move it directly to Code view. Then you can use the upgraded code-hinting feature that supports XML and XSLT to change the code according to your needs.

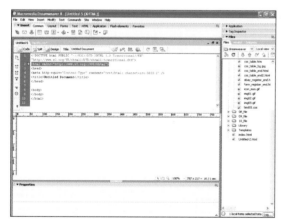

Basic XML format

16

Integration with Fireworks for Image Editing

Photoshop is the most frequently used program for creating or editing images to be inserted into Web pages. Macromedia Fireworks is another excellent program for this purpose. Unlike Photoshop, Fireworks is exclusively for creating images for the Web and is very convenient to use for producing Web-page content. Since Fireworks is integrated with Dreamweaver, you can use its various editing features while using Dreamweaver. This means that you can perform simple image-editing jobs in Dreamweaver without running a separate graphics program. To use these features, you must have both Fireworks and Dreamweaver installed. You can then use Firework's image-optimization and Web gallery features in Dreamweaver.

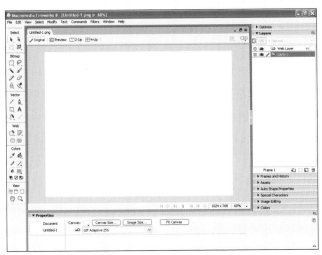

Fireworks

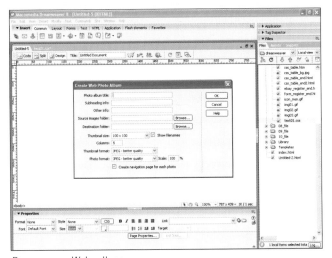

Dreamweaver Web gallery

Integration with Contribute for User Synchronization

Contribute is another Adobe/Macromedia program that allows groups of people to collectively update Web sites through an easy-to-use browser interface. This can be invaluable when it comes to keeping large sites up-to-date. Dreamweaver offers excellent integration and support for Contribute users.

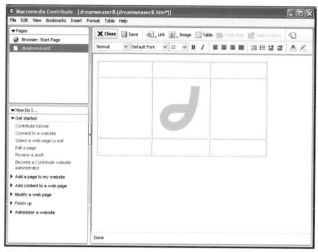

Contribute dialog box

Integration with Flash for Flash Videos

Macromedia's Flash, the most popular program for creating Web animations, is an indispensable element of Dreamweaver. It has always been integrated with Dreamweaver, and with the upgraded version, Flash video features in Dreamweaver have become more powerful than ever before.

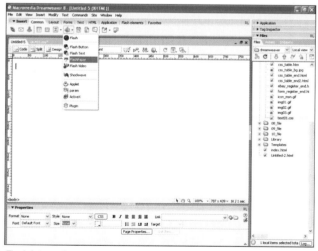

Flash integration

Background File Transfer

You can continue working with Dreamweaver 8 even while files are being uploaded to a server. For example, using this new feature, you can work with files in a local system while Dreamweaver is communicating with the server.

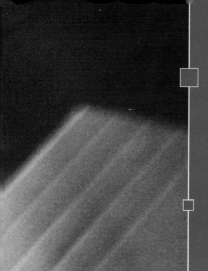

Working in Dreamweaver

Dreamweaver 8 offers a highly intuitive interface to ensure that beginners and veterans, designers and programmers alike can get the most from the program. In this section, we'll introduce the Dreamweaver work environment, then walk you through creating a local site (a crucial first step toward working in Dreamweaver).

The Dreamweaver 8 Interface

This section describes the interface of Dreamweaver 8, which allows for fast insertion, placement, and editing of contents.

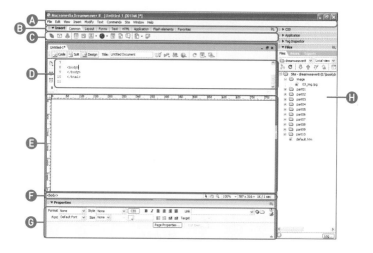

Ⓐ Menu bar: Contains all the menus and features used in Dreamweaver.

Ⓑ Insert bar: Contains buttons for inserting various types of objects into a document.

Ⓒ Document toolbar: Contains buttons that provide options for document views and properties.

Ⓓ Code inspector: Shows the contents of Design view as HTML code.

Ⓔ Document window: Also called Design view or the work window, the Document window allows you to create HTML documents as if drawing a picture.

Ⓕ Tag selector: Allows you to directly select desired HTML tags with a mouse click.

Ⓖ Properties inspector: Allows you to set and manage the properties of objects inserted in a document.

Ⓗ Panel groups: Gathers together sets of related panels used for various features such as page management. All panels can be managed from the Window menu.

Work Window Layouts

You can perform coding and design jobs at the same time within Dreamweaver by selecting a work window layout. Dreamweaver provides three work window layouts from which you can choose, as needed.

Code view

Design view

Split view

The Menu Bar

Dreamweaver's Menu bar contains numerous commands grouped together into menus according to function. It's not necessary to memorize every command, but you should have a basic idea of what each menu does.

The Insert Bar

The Insert bar contains buttons for inserting various objects (such as text and Flash elements) into the work window. There are two display options: Show as Menu and Show as Tabs. The default setting is Show as Menu, but the setting can be toggled directly from the Insert bar. The functions offered are the same regardless of the display choice, so you can select whichever option is most convenient for you.

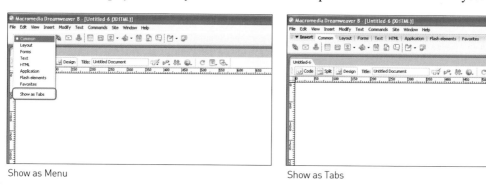

Show as Menu   Show as Tabs

Ⓐ **Common**: Allows you to insert the most commonly used objects for creating pages, such as images and tables.

Ⓑ **Layout**: Allows you to insert tables, div tags, layers, and frames. You can also choose among three table views: Standard (default), Expanded Tables, and Layout. When Layout mode is selected, you can use the Dreamweaver layout tools: Layout Cell and Draw Layout Table.

C **Forms**: Contains buttons for selecting and inserting the form styles that are required to create forms.

D **Text**: Allows you to insert various text- and list-formatting tags.

E **HTML**: Allows you to insert HTML tags for horizontal rules, head content, tables, frames, and scripts.

F **Application**: This feature can be applied to pages that use specific server languages such as ASP, ASP.NET, CFML Basic and Advanced, JSP, and PHP. Each of these categories provides server code objects that can be inserted in Code view. Using the Application category allows you to insert dynamic elements such as record sets, repeated regions, and record insertion and update forms.

G **Flash elements**: Allows you to insert high-quality Flash slide images (bitmap only).

H **Favorites**: Allows you to group and organize in one place the Insert bar buttons that you use most often.

The Document Toolbar

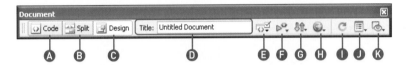

A **Show Code View**: Displays only the Code view in the Document window.

B **Show Split View**: Displays both Code and Design views in the Document window.

C **Show Design View**: Displays only the Design view in the Document window.

D **Title**: Allows you to enter a title for your document.

E **No Browser/Check Errors**: Allows you to check browser compatibility.

F **File Management**: Displays the File Management pop-up menu.

G **Validate Markup**: Checks for errors from HTML code to JavaServer page tags (i.e., validates them).

H **Preview/Debug in Browser**: Allows you to preview or debug your document in a browser. Select a browser from the pop-up menu or press the F12 key.

I **Refresh Design View**: Refreshes the Design view to show the changes made in Code view.

J **View Options**: Allows you to set view options for the Document window. You can select the view mode for visual elements and rulers as well as grid options.

K **Visual Aids**: Allows you to show/hide image maps, table widths and borders, and layers in the work window.

Panels

As with most graphics programs, panels in Dreamweaver are essentially embedded windows that offer quick access to specialized functions. For instance, the Behaviors panel allows you to conveniently apply behaviors to the work window. Through panels you can apply advanced features to objects and easily manage and transfer files, objects, CSSs, Java scripts, and server scripts. Since panels occupy space, they may sometimes get in your way. If this is the case, you can place a required panel in a more convenient position or you can hide a specific panel or all panels.

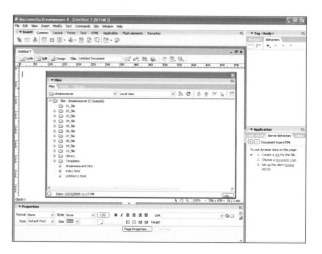

Panel Groups

Ⓐ To maximize or minimize a panel group, click the maximization arrow (▶) at the left of the panel group's title bar or click the title of the panel group.

Ⓑ To close a panel group and hide it from the window, select Close Panel Group from the Options menu on the panel group's title bar (this appears only when it is maximized).

Ⓒ To view the Options menu for the panel group, click the title or maximization arrow to maximize the panel group. The Options menu can be seen only when the panel group is maximized.

Ⓓ To open a panel group or a panel hidden from the window, select the panel group or panel from the Window menu. The items that are not checked in the Window menu are currently open. The items may not be visible because they are hidden behind another window.

The Tag Selector and Status Bar

Ⓐ **Tag Selector**: The Tag Selector shows the hierarchy of tags surrounding the current selection. When you click a tag in the hierarchy, that tag and its contents are selected. You can also select the entire body of the document by clicking <body>.

Ⓑ **Select tool**: Click the Select tool to disable the Zoom or Hand tools.

Ⓒ **Hand tool**: When the document is magnified with the Zoom tool and only part of it is shown, you can use the Hand tool instead of the scroll bar to move around within it. Dragging the document with the mouse enables you to see every hidden part of it.

Ⓓ **Zoom tool**: Allows you to magnify or shrink your document by clicking it with the mouse. You can zoom out by clicking the document while pressing the Alt key.

Ⓔ **Set magnification**: Allows you to set a magnification level for your document.

Ⓕ **Window Size pop-up menu**: Allows you to resize the Document window according to the browser size optimized for the monitor resolution. You can resize it to the predetermined size or to custom dimensions that you define.

Ⓖ **Document size and estimated download time**: To the right of the Window Size pop-up menu are the size and estimated download time for the document. These numbers take into account all dependent files, such as images and other media files. They can be seen in the Design view only. Using the Window Size pop-up menu allows you to resize the Document window to predetermined or custom dimensions.

The Properties Inspector

The Properties inspector enables you to view and edit frequently used properties for a selected page element. Different properties appear in the Properties inspector depending on the kind of element selected, such as text, image, layer, frame, or Flash. The Properties inspector is displayed at the bottom of the work window by default, but you can change its position if you want. To move the Properties inspector, click its top-left corner and drag it.

Setting Up a Local Site

Before getting started with the production of a Web site that consists of one or many HTML documents, you need to set up a specific space for your work in Dreamweaver. This is not just a matter of allocating space; setting up a local site allows you to manage various documents and objects and quickly apply them prior to the online transfer stage. Site setup also supports a collaborative work environment. For instance, when Web designers and programmers work together on a Web site, they can set up a site as one Web server, which they can work on and manage simultaneously from different locations.

Local Site
\Sample\

Site Definition

The basic objective of site definition in Dreamweaver is to speed up the work process. Defining a site offers the benefit of automatic creation and modification of paths when adding objects and links in a page. Moreover, since some features require a site definition, it is an essential step. Defining a site means that you declare a work space and use additional features such as FTP and local site when creating a Web site through a project. You need to perform site definition only once when starting a project.

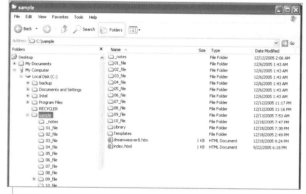

1 First, copy the example files on the enclosed CD to your C: drive and decompress them. The location of your work files must now be set as your local site in Dreamweaver.

2 Open Dreamweaver and click Manage Sites in the File panel on the right.

3 When the Manage Sites dialog box opens, click New and then Site in the menu that appears.

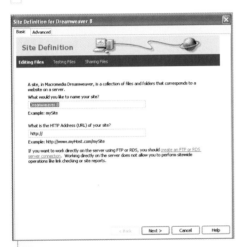

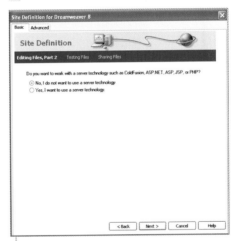

4 You can define a local site for a Web programmer or designer. If you'll be using a Web server, it is a good idea to define a site after setting up the Web server. When the dialog box opens, as shown in the figure, click the Basic tab, then enter "Dreamweaver 8" and click the Next button.

5 The next page asks whether or not you want to use server technology in your Web site. Select "No, I do not want to use a server technology" and click the Next button.

tip >>

Site Management

When you want to save a site definition, you can use the Export feature from Manage Sites to save the *.ste file. The *.ste file is written in XML format as shown here.

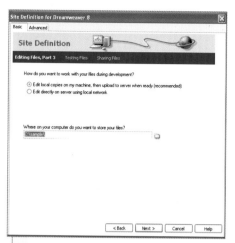

6　Now you should define the file path for your local site. Select the location in which you've placed the example files from the enclosed CD and click the Next button. Here we will select the folder C:\sample.

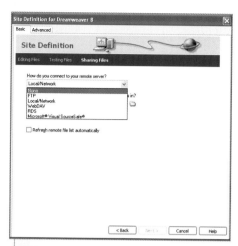

7　Configure the remote server. At this time, select None and click the Next button.

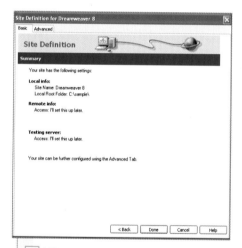

8　When you've completed all the settings, you can review them again. If everything is OK, click the Done button to finish site definition.

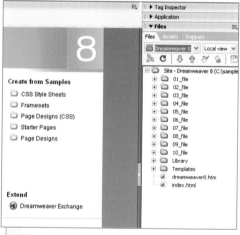

9　You can check the list of setup sites from the Files panel as shown here.

tip >>

Configuration of the remote server is one of the strengths of Dreamweaver. Typically you should use an FTP (File Transfer Protocol) program to interact with a Web server. However, the remote server setting of Dreamweaver allows direct FTP connection, so you don't need a separate FTP program. With the remote server setting you can upload and download files in real time with the Web server. For this reason, you have to take special care not to expose the wrong information to visitors; even though removing the intermediate step of checking finished documents before uploading them to the Web server offers the benefit of speed, it has the shortcoming of providing no feedback for author errors. When Web designers configure a remote server using FTP, it is recommended they use it only for basic FTP features rather than real-time uploading and downloading.

Site Modification

You can modify a setup site using the Manage Sites menu.

1 │ Click Manage Sites from the File panel.

2 │ Select a site to modify from the Manage Sites dialog box. Then click the Edit button.

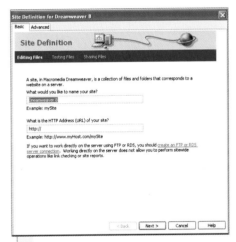

3 │ The Site Definition dialog box appears, and you can change the contents as required.

---

tip >>

Web Programming in Dreamweaver

Web designers work in HTML to produce the look and feel of Web sites. Web programmers work in *.asp or *.php to create the underlying server technology that runs complicated Web sites. In the past, these roles have been separate and well defined, but this is changing as design and programming tools add new features that "cross the line" into each other's territory. Dreamweaver in particular now offers quite a list of features to entice programmers, and for this reason the decision to include server technology when defining local sites will vary depending on the user and the goal for the Web site.

Chapter | 2

Working with Text and Images

Text and images are the most basic elements of Web pages. These components are used to provide information and draw viewers into sites. This chapter explains how to insert, arrange, and edit this content conveniently in Dreamweaver. If you have used a word-processing program before, this aspect of Dreamweaver will be no problem.

Adding Text and Images to a Web Page

I n this section we'll introduce Dreamweaver's text and graphic tools. We'll then take on several exercises designed to get you comfortable with inserting and configuring these elements in your Web pages.

Inserting Text

You can insert text with your keyboard immediately after starting Dreamweaver. You can directly change the size, format, and style of text just as you would in a word-processing program. To insert text into a document in Dreamweaver, simply move the mouse cursor to Design view or Code view and type the text into the document.

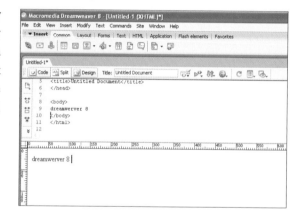

The Text Properties Inspector

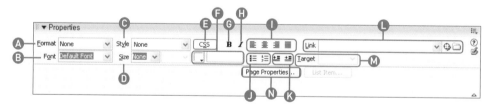

Ⓐ **Format**: Apply the selected text property using the <H> tag.

Ⓑ **Font**: You can change the font of the text you've inserted using any of the fonts installed on your PC. If there are only basic fonts in this font list and you wish to add fonts that are not listed, click Edit Font List and add the new fonts.

Ⓒ **Style**: You can apply a CSS style to selected text by choosing from the style list.

Ⓓ **Size**: You can specify the text size from 1 to 7. The larger the number, the greater the text size. Use + to apply a size that's larger, relative to the current text size.

Ⓔ **CSS**: Click this icon to call up the CSS panel.

F **Text Color**: Select a text color. You can click the icon to select a color from the color list. Alternatively, directly input a hexadecimal color code into the text field.

G **Bold**: Changes the text to Bold style.

H **Italic**: Changes the text to Italic style.

I **Alignment**: Specifies the alignment of text—Left, Center, Right, or Mixed alignment—from left to right.

J **List**: Inserts a bullet symbol or number in front of each selected paragraph to create nonsequential or sequential lists.

K **Text Outdent/Text Indent**: Applies an outdent or indent to the selected paragraph.

L **Hyperlink**: Applies a link to the selected text. There are three methods for setting a hyperlink: directly entering a filename to link to, dragging and dropping the Print to File icon to the file you wish to link to, and selecting a file to link to by clicking the Browse for File icon.

M **Target**: Allows you to select whether a hyperlinked page will be displayed in a new window or the current window. The following options are available:

_blank: The linked document appears in a new browser.

_self: The linked document opens in the current browser.

_parent: The linked document opens in the parent frame set of the current frame.

_top: The linked document opens in the current browser regardless of the frame structure.

N **Page Properties**: Opens the dialog box for setting the properties of the work page.

Working with Fonts

All programs recognize system fonts during startup, and you can often use these fonts in an unrestricted manner. However, Dreamweaver may not read all the fonts in the operating system because it recognizes only the most basic fonts. The program is written this way to prevent the use of user-specific fonts in Dreamweaver output. If a Web-page visitor who does not have the Arial font, for example, visits a Web site that uses that font, the appearance and overall layout of the document may not look to the visitor as the producer intended.

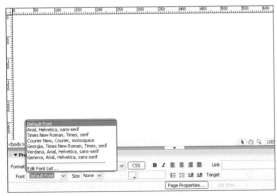

Basic default fonts

There are two solutions that are most often used to get around this issue. The first solution is to convert text to an image. To use special fonts, you can use a graphics program such as Photoshop to save text elements as images and then insert these images into documents.

The second solution is to use Web fonts, which allow for the use of special fonts without requiring that Web viewers have them installed on their systems. This offers the benefit of producing more varied text styles on Web sites and of reducing the page size, but one disadvantage is that you need to buy Web fonts.

To add fonts to Dreamweaver, click Edit Font List from the Font menu in the Properties inspector. Select the desired fonts in Available fonts and move them to Chosen fonts by pressing the arrow button, then click OK to finalize your selections.

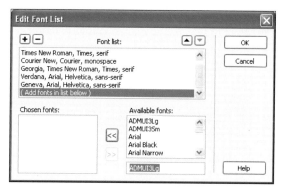 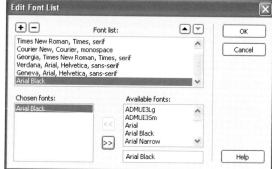

Adding Images

To insert an image, move the mouse cursor to the desired position and choose Common > Image in the Insert bar. When the Select Image Source dialog box appears, you can insert the desired images.

The work document must be saved in order for the image path to be specified as a relative path (i.e., a path "sourced" to the work document's file structure). If the document into which you are inserting an image is not saved, Dreamweaver shows a warning message and inserts the image as an absolute path (i.e., a path sourced to your hard drive directory).

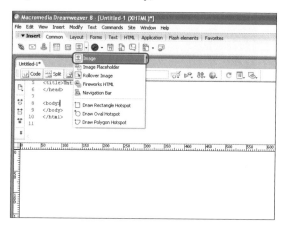 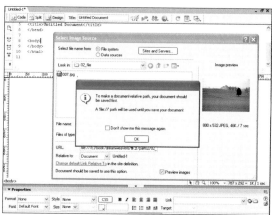

The Image Properties Inspector

This panel is used to set the properties of images in a document. You can edit the image properties by selecting an image.

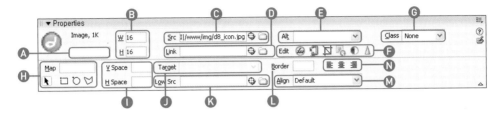

Ⓐ Image name: When an image is inserted, its name is not defined by default. However, images must be named if they are going to be used with behaviors or JavaScript, which are object-oriented.

Ⓑ W/H: Specifies the height and width of the image.

Ⓒ Src: Indicates the image path.

Ⓓ Link: Indicates the location of the document linked to the image.

Ⓔ Alt: Allows you to add supplementary information to an image. This info appears as a balloon when viewers place their mouses over the image in the Web browser.

Ⓕ Edit: Allows you to perform simple image-editing jobs using some features of Fireworks (an editing program specialized for Web images), such as optimizing, cropping, resizing, adjusting the brightness and contrast, and sharpening an image.

Ⓖ Class: Applies a style sheet.

Ⓗ Map: This is used to set several links to one image. You may give a rectangular, circular, or polygonal shape to the linked parts.

Ⓘ V Space/H Space: Sets the vertical and horizontal spacing for images.

Ⓙ Target: Select a link type for the image.

blank: The linked document appears in a new browser.

self: The linked document opens in the current browser.

parent: The linked document opens in the parent frame set of the current frame.

top: The linked document opens in the current browser regardless of the frame structure.

Ⓚ Low Src: Sets a preview image. If the image size is large or the Internet speed of the Web site visitor is slow, it takes a long time for the image to load. In this case, you can specify that a low-resolution image will show until the original image appears.

Ⓛ Border: Specifies the thickness of the image border. Even though the image border is black, it changes to blue by default when it is linked.

Ⓜ Align: Select an alignment method when images and text are mixed.

Ⓝ Alignment: Aligns images to the left, center, or right.

Dreamweaver is primarily a program for creating, managing, and editing HTML. However, since Web pages almost always include graphics, Dreamweaver facilitates use of some Fireworks features for editing images. For professional-quality image editing, you should use a specialized image-editing program such as Photoshop or Fireworks. However, simple editing jobs can be performed within Dreamweaver.

Optimizing Image Size

For Web-based work, it is very important to optimize image size to ensure maximum image quality while maintaining fast transfer speeds. Both Fireworks and Photoshop allow you save images optimized for Web use.

Crop

The crop feature allows you to highlight an area of an image, then trim the areas of the graphic that fall outside the selection. This is a method used often in photography to alter the focal point of an image or reduce the size of the background. Needless to say, it can be critical when preparing graphics for the Web.

To crop an image, start by clicking the Crop icon from the Properties inspector. Once the icon is clicked, a selection box will appear over the graphic. By moving the eight points along the edge of the selection box, you can set the desired area to be cropped (anything outside the selection box will be cropped from the graphic). Press enter to finalize your selection and crop the image.

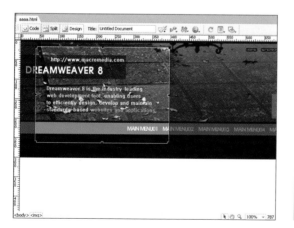
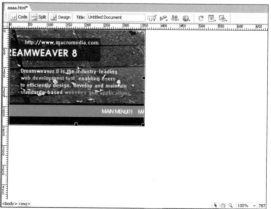

Resamples

When images are inserted into Web pages, their dimensions are usually fixed. In other words, they appear at their "natural" size by default. As a result, the dimensions of your graphic files will play a key role in the layout of your pages (this is particularly important when inserting graphics into tables, as table cells will automatically adjust to the size of their embedded graphics). Normally, dedicated graphics programs such as Photoshop or Fireworks would be used to resize images, but Dreamweaver offers a resampling function to do this within the program. After selecting an image, simply input the desired W (Width) and H (Height) in the Properties inspector, then click on the Resample icon.

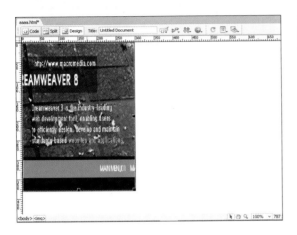 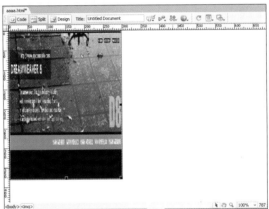

Brightness and Contrast

Rather than requiring you to use additional image-editing software, Dreamweaver allows you to alter the brightness and contrast of your images within the program. After selecting an image, click the Brightness/Contrast icon from the Properties inspector. Once the Brightness/Contrast dialog box appears, you can change the brightness and/or contrast by moving the corresponding slider.

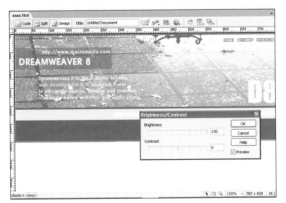 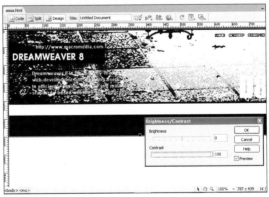

Brightness

Contrast

Sharpen

Sharpening an image brings it into better focus, as shown below. To do so, select an image and click the Sharpen icon from the Properties inspector. Once the Sharpen dialog box appears, you can change the sharpness of the image by moving the slider.

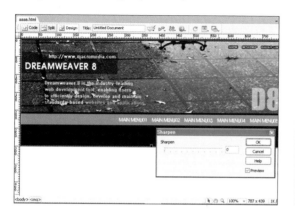 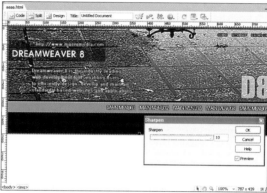

Using an External Image Editor

If Dreamweaver lacks the image-editing functionality you require, you can easily access an external editor from within Dreamweaver. Review the following steps to set this up.

1. You can select an external image editor from the Preferences dialog box. Although Fireworks is the default image-editing program, you can change the default to Photoshop or other programs. To make this change, select Preferences from the Edit menu and click File Types/Editors in the Category list.

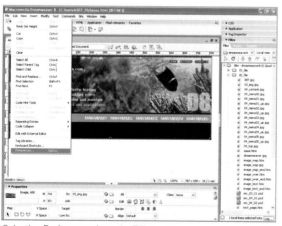

Selecting Preferences from the Edit menu

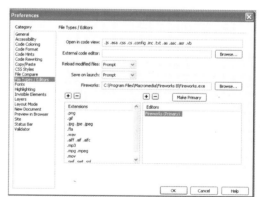

Preferences dialog box

2. You can see that Fireworks is set as the default program in File Types/Editors. If Fireworks is not installed on your PC, another graphics program that has been installed will have been set as the default.

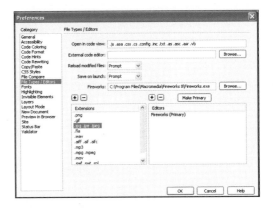

3. Select Fireworks from Editors and click the ⊟ button to remove it as the default.

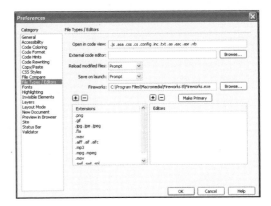

4. To set Photoshop as the default image-editing program, click the ⊞ button above Editors, select Photoshop, and then click the OK button.

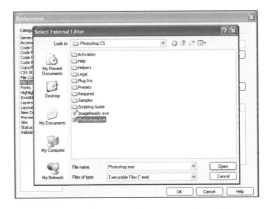

5. You can see that the Photoshop program is now the default image editor.

Creating a Text-Based Web Page

Web site design is changing rapidly with the development of more and more Web sites. Increasing Internet speed is enabling the use of multimedia content such as Flash animation and video. Moreover, new text formats are being researched and developed. In this exercise we'll create a text-based Web page to illustrate the text handling features of Dreamweaver.

Source File
> \Sample\02_file\text.txt

Saved File
> \Sample\02_file\text_page.htm

Final File
> \Sample\02_file\text_page_end.htm

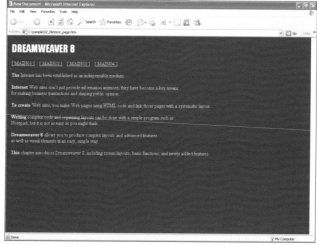

Final page

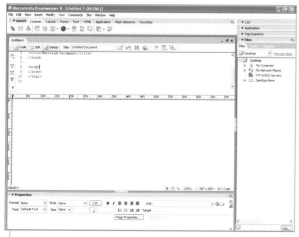

1 | Start Dreamweaver and click Create New > HTML.

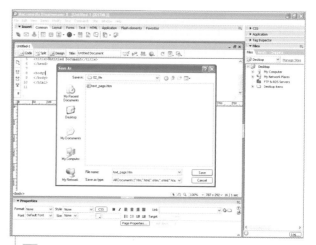

2 | Choose File > Save to save the current page. Here we will save it as \Sample\02_file\text_page.htm.

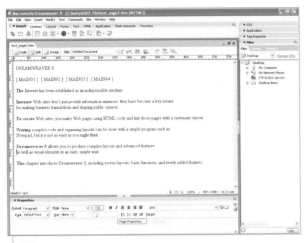

tip >>

The <P> tag and the <BR> tag

In HTML, you use the <P> tag and <BR> tag paragraphs and lines, respectively. In Dreamweaver, it is most convenient to use the keyboard to insert the <P> and <BR> tags rather than inserting them from the Insert panel.

<P>: In Design view, place the mouse cursor at the insertion point and press the Enter key on your keyboard to insert a new line.

: In Design view, place the mouse cursor at the insertion point and press the Shift-Enter keys on your keyboard to insert a new line.

Note that you should not use the <P> tag repeatedly (as in "<P><P><P><P><P>"), but you can use the <BR> tag repeatedly (as in "

").

3 Insert text as shown here. For this text, use the contents of the \Sample\02_file\text.txt file.

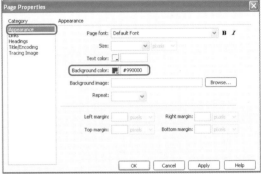

4 First, we will set #990000 as the background color of the page. Click Page Properties in the Properties inspector or click Ctrl-J. When the Page Properties dialog box appears, enter #990000 in Background color of the Appearance section and then click OK.

tip >>

Text Settings in Dreamweaver

Dreamweaver controls text through cascading style sheets (CSSs), which allow you to save and apply text formatting styles. If there were no CSSs, you would have to format everything in a document, from font type to size to style, individually.

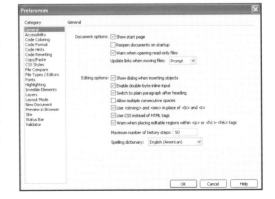

Dreamweaver offers automatic CSS settings. However, you may need to customize styles according to the specific purpose of each Web site. To deactivate the automatic CSS setting in Dreamweaver, choose Edit > Preferences. Then select General under Category and uncheck the Use CSS instead of HTML tags option.

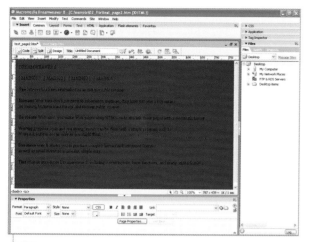

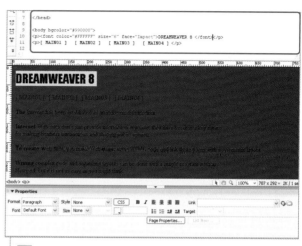

5 You can see that the background color of the page has changed.

6 Select "DREAMWEAVER 8" at the top of the document using with your mouse. Then select Impact for font, #FFFFFF for color, and 6 for text size in the Properties inspector.

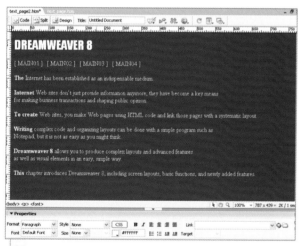

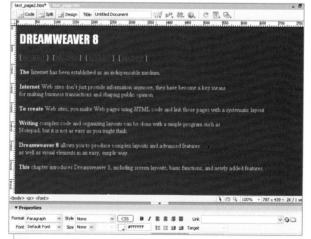

7 Now change the color for the rest of the text to #FFFFFF.

8 Next, add links to each of the menu items: MAIN01, MAIN02, MAIN03, and MAIN04. To add a link to MAIN01, select it and enter a link (or input "#" in the Link field of the Properties inspector). Add links to other menu items in the same manner. You can see the menu texts are underlined now, showing that they are linked.

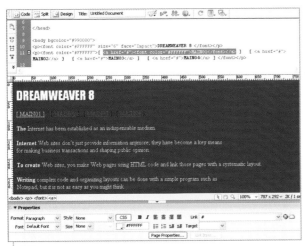

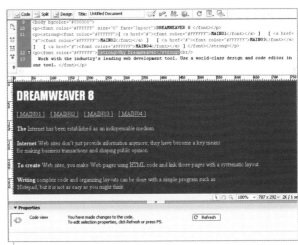

9 You can change the color of linked text if you want. Let's select the linked texts and change their color to #FFFFFF. It is a good idea here to click the Split view button and directly change the text color in the HTML. See the sample coding below for reference.

```
<a href="#"><font color="#FFFFFF">MAIN01
</font></a>
<a href="#"><font color="#FFFFFF">MAIN02
</font></a>
<a href="#"><font color="#FFFFFF">MAIN03
</font></a>
<a href="#"><font color="#FFFFFF">MAIN04
</font></a>
```

10 Now select each of the titles and menus in the text and apply bold by clicking the Bold icon in the Properties inspector. Notice that the <strong> tag appears, not the <B> tag.

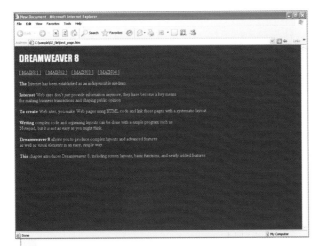

11 Save the edited text and press the F12 key on your keyboard to preview it.

The Impact font is not specified as a standard font in Dreamweaver, so you should add it using the font-adding method described here.

❶ Click Edit Font List from Font in the Properties inspector.

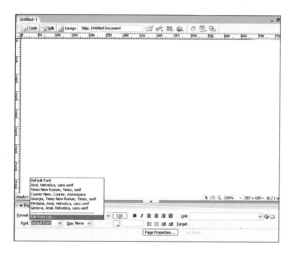

❷ Select the Impact font in the Edit Font List dialog box. With the Impact font selected, click the left arrow icon.

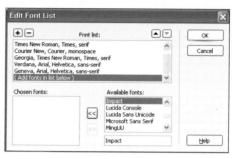

❸ Note that the Impact font is added as shown in the figure below. Click the OK button to save the setting.

❹ You can see that the Impact font has been added to the Font list in the Properties inspector.

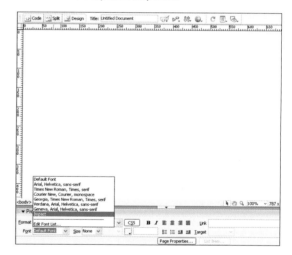

Configuring Images and Text

Web site text delivers information to visitors, but you can also deliver information with images and visual effects. In this exercise, we will insert images and text into Web pages and align these two types of content to ensure they work together.

Source File
    \Sample\02_file\dreamweaver.jpg

Start File
    \Sample\02_file\image_text.htm

Final File
    \Sample\02_file\image_text_end.htm

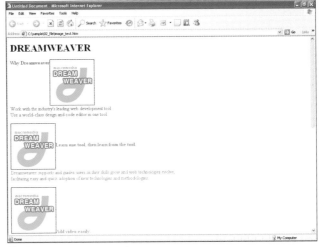

Final page

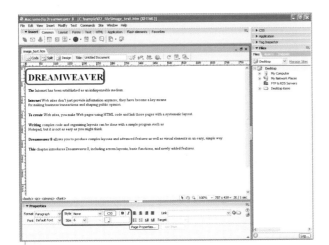

1 Open the \Sample\02_file\ image_text.htm file. Select the text "DREAMWEAVER" as a block. Then set the text size to 6 and apply Bold styling from the Properties inspector.

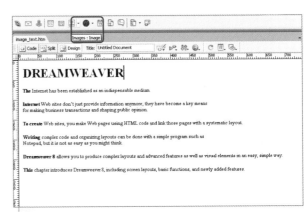

2 Move the mouse cursor to the first title and choose Common > Image from the Insert bar.

3 Select the dreamweaver.jpg file in the Select Image Source dialog box. Then click OK.

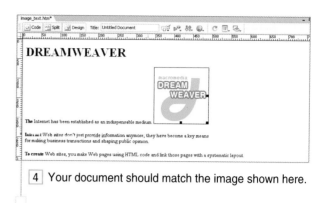

4 Your document should match the image shown here.

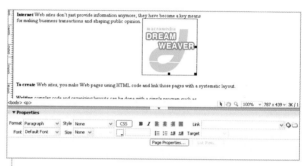

5 Select the image and choose Align > Top in the Properties inspector. The text moves up to align with the top of the image.

6 Insert the graphic for each of the other titles using the same method. Specify a different text color for each paragraph to set them apart.

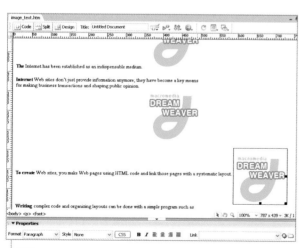

7 Modify the Align setting to complete the page. The Align feature allows you to align each grouping of image and text differently. The most frequently used styles are Top, Middle, and Bottom.

8 Save the edited page and press the F12 key on your keyboard to preview it.

The Image Tag Accessibility Attributes Dialog Box

When you insert an image in Dreamweaver, the Image Tag Accessibility Attributes dialog box opens by default. This allows you to alter the initial settings for an image. However, as the dialog box appears repeatedly whenever you insert an image, it is recommended that you set preferences so that it will not appear by default. To hide the Image Tag Accessibility Attributes dialog box, you should deactivate the feature in the Dreamweaver preferences, as shown below.

❶ Choose Edit > Preferences or press Ctrl-U.

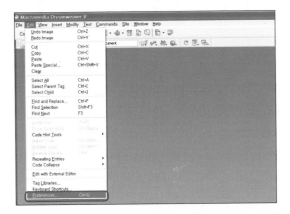

❷ When the Preferences dialog box appears, click the Accessibility category in the Category menu.

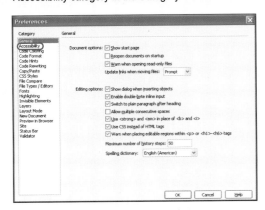

❸ You can see the settings for the Accessibility category at right.

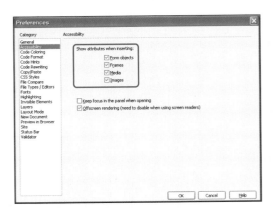

❹ Uncheck Images under Show attributes when inserting, and click the OK button. From now on when you insert an image in Dreamweaver, the Image Tag Accessibility Attributes dialog box will not open. If you uncheck the boxes for Form Objects, Frames, or Media, the Tag Accessibility Attributes dialog box for these won't open either.

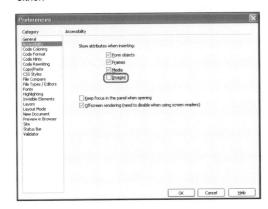

3 Using Image Maps to Add Links to Images

You can add links to text and images that allow users to move from the current document to another document or Web site. Using image maps, which have rectangular, circular, or polygonal shapes, Dreamweaver goes a step further by allowing you to isolate specific areas of an image for linking. In this exercise, we'll show you how it's done.

Final page

Start File
\Sample\02_file\image_map.htm

Final File
\Sample\02_file\image_map_end.htm

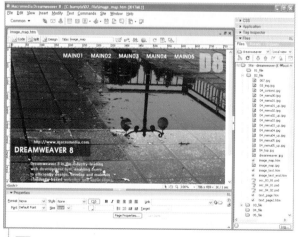

[1] Open the \sample\02_file\image_map.htm file. You can see that an image has been placed in the document.

[2] Click the image. The Properties inspector now shows the image's properties.

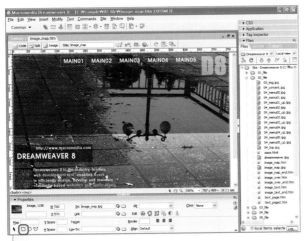

3 With the image selected, click the Rectangular Hotspot tool in the Properties inspector. Drag a box around MAIN01 with your mouse, as shown here.

4 When you activate an image map, the Properties inspector shows image map settings, as shown here.

5 Minimize the panel groups to make the Document window wider. With the image map selected, click a blank space in Design view to release the Rectangular Hotspot tool.

tip >>

The Hotspot Properties Inspector

A **Link**: Enter a link address; when the image map area is clicked in a Web browser, it will link to this address.

B **Target**: This setting determines how the hyperlink will behave in Web browsers. Choose from Blank, Parent, Self, and Top.

C **Alt**: When the mouse pointer is positioned in the image map area (when viewing the page in a browser), a help balloon appears. You can enter the text for this balloon here.

D **Map**: Specify a name for the image map.

49

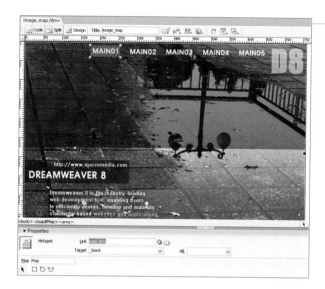

6 Drag the resize handles at each corner of the image map to change its shape. Specify the link in the Properties inspector. Here, we will link to main.htm.

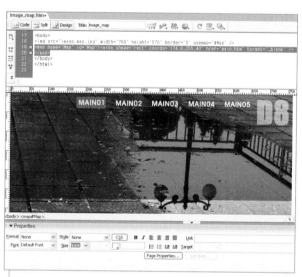

7 Click the Split button and check the HTML in Code view. See the sample code below for reference.

8 Set image maps for the other menu options using the same technique. Sample code is given below.

```
<img    src="image_map.jpg"    width="760"
height="570" border="0" usemap="#Map" />
<map name="Map" id="Map">
<area  shape="rect"  coords="174,8,255,40"
href="main.htm" target="_blank" />
</map>
```

```
<map name="Map" id="Map">
   <area  shape="rect"  coords="570,10,655,40"
href="main5.htm" target="_blank" />
   <area  shape="rect"  coords="470,10,555,40"
href="main4.htm" target="_blank" />
   <area  shape="rect"  coords="370,10,455,40"
href="main3.htm" target="_blank" />
   <area  shape="rect"  coords="270,10,355,40"
href="main2.htm" target="_blank" />
   <area  shape="rect"  coords="170,10,255,40"
href="main1.htm" target="_blank" />
</map>
```

50

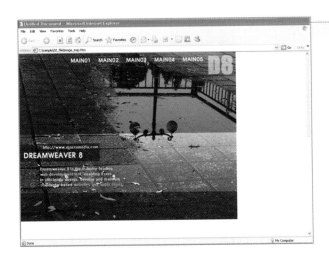

9 Save the edited document and press the F12 key on your keyboard to preview it.

Selecting and Modifying an Image Map

Selecting an image map area using the freehand method is not the best way to ensure a precise selection. Generally, it is better to apply the image map and then modify it to increase the accuracy of its area of effect.

To change the shape of an image map, click in a blank space in Design view to release the Rectangular Hotspot tool. Then select the image map to open the Hotspot Properties inspector. You will also see resize handles at each corner of the selected image map, as shown here. You can change the shape of the map or move it by clicking and dragging the resize handles. You can also use the arrow keys on your keyboard to move the image map more subtly, because the arrow keys on the keyboard allow you to move the image map in one-pixel increments.

Creating a Rollover Menu Using Images

You can see menus and content created with Flash animation on many Web sites. Flash is a technology for producing highly dynamic Web sites. But you don't have to use Flash to achieve similar effects; you can create interactive menus with JavaScript. The most frequently used interactive menus are rollover menus that respond to a mouse event. In this exercise, we will create a rollover menu in which image changes are triggered by the mouse.

Source Folder
\Sample\02_file\

Start File
\Sample\02_file\image_over.htm

Final File
\Sample\02_file\image_over_end.htm

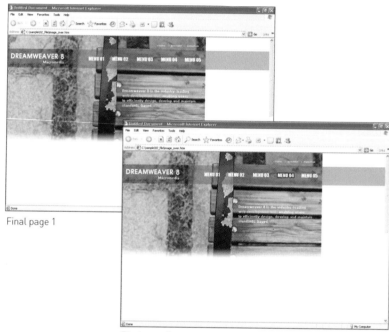

Final page 1

Final page 2

1 Open the \Sample\02_file\image_over.htm file.

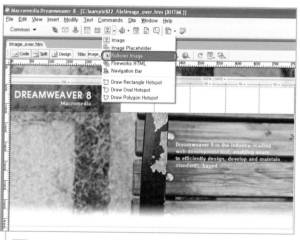

2 Now we will add a menu to a blank table. Position your mouse pointer over the first cell of the blank table. Choose Common > Image in the Insert bar and then click Rollover Image.

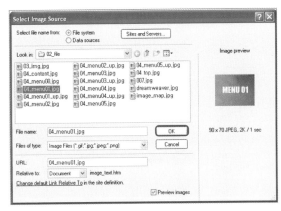

3 When the Insert Rollover Image dialog box opens, click the Browse button next to Original image. Select the 04_menu01.jpg file in the Select Image Source dialog box. Then click OK.

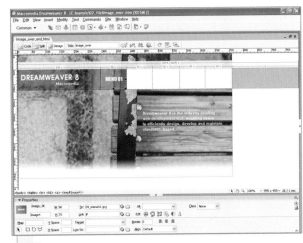

4 In the Insert Rollover Image dialog box, click the Browse button next to Rollover image. Insert the image 04_menu01_up.jpg and click the OK button.

5 You can see that the MENU 01 image has been inserted into the document as shown here.

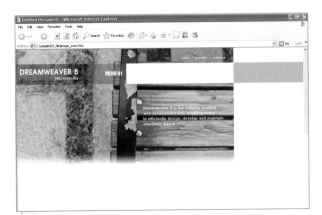

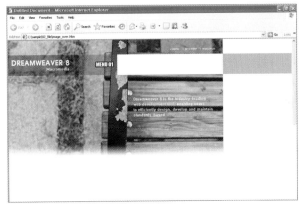

6 Save the edited document. Click F12 to preview it and verify that the menu rollover works.

7 In this way you can easily create rollover menus. However, the actual HTML source is not so simple. Click the Split button to see the inserted source. This is why Dreamweaver is so handy!

8 Insert other menu items in the same manner.

Button	Original Image	Rollover Image
MENU 02	04_menu02.jpg	04_menu02_up.jpg
MENU 03	04_menu03.jpg	04_menu03_up.jpg
MENU 04	04_menu04.jpg	04_menu04_up.jpg
MENU 05	04_menu05.jpg	04_menu05_up.jpg

```
<script type="text/JavaScript">
<!
function MM_swapImgRestore() { //v3.0
  var i,x,a=document.MM_sr; for(i=0;a&&i<a.length&&(x=a[i])&&x.oSrc;i++) x.src=x.oSrc;
}

function MM_preloadImages() { //v3.0
  var d=document; if(d.images){ if(!d.MM_p) d.MM_p=new Array();
    var i,j=d.MM_p.length,a=MM_preloadImages.arguments; for(i=0; i<a.length; i++)
    if (a[i].indexOf("#")!=0){ d.MM_p[j]=new Image; d.MM_p[j++].src=a[i];}}
}

function MM_findObj(n, d) { //v4.01
  var p,i,x;  if(!d) d=document; if((p=n.indexOf("?"))>0&&parent.frames.length) {
    d=parent.frames[n.substring(p+1)].document; n=n.substring(0,p);}
  if(!(x=d[n])&&d.all) x=d.all[n]; for (i=0;!x&&i<d.forms.length;i++) x=d.forms[i][n];
  for(i=0;!x&&d.layers&&i<d.layers.length;i++) x=MM_findObj(n,d.layers[i].document);
  if(!x && d.getElementById) x=d.getElementById(n); return x;
}

function MM_swapImage() { //v3.0
  var i,j=0,x,a=MM_swapImage.arguments; document.MM_sr=new Array; for(i=0;i<(a.length 2);i+=3)
  if ((x=MM_findObj(a[i]))!=null){document.MM_sr[j++]=x; if(!x.oSrc) x.oSrc=x.src; x.src=a[i+2];}
}
//   >
</script>
```

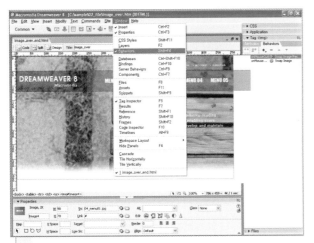 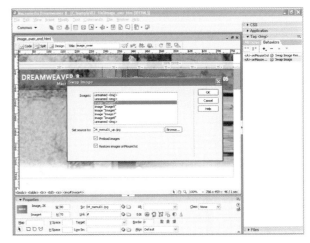

9 To change an inserted image, choose Behaviors from the Window menu. When the Behaviors panel opens at right, double-click Swap Image.

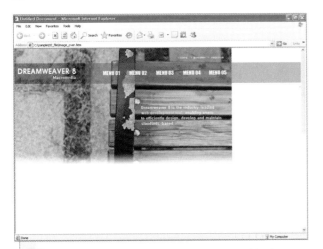 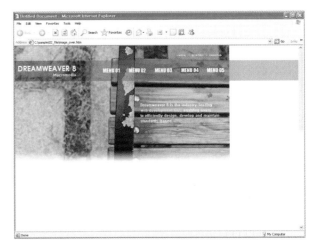

10 Save the edited document and press the F12 key on your keyboard to preview it in a Web browser.

Chapter 3

Using Tables to Build Pages

On a basic level, tables are useful for aligning objects such as text, graphics, and Flash elements. Advanced users, however, know that tables can be used effectively to construct entire Web pages. In this chapter we'll start with a brief intro to table basics, then explore the full potential of tables through a series of advanced exercises.

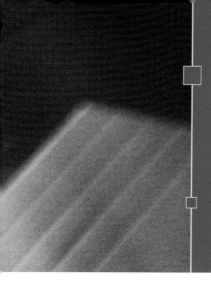

The Basic Properties of Tables

A Web page primarily consists of text and images, which you can position systematically by using tables. Tables in a Web page are comparable to the support structures in a house; the table itself provides the frame for your layout, while the contents of each cell create the overall look and feel of your page. To get things started, let's review Dreamweaver's extensive set of table features.

What Is a Table?

A table is an object in itself, but it is more often used as a framework for positioning or arranging other objects in a Web page. The most important role of tables is to provide a framework for defining the layout of a Web page. As such, tables are one of the most important elements of Web pages, and you should understand their properties in order to use them properly. The basic structure of a table composed of HTML tags is shown below.

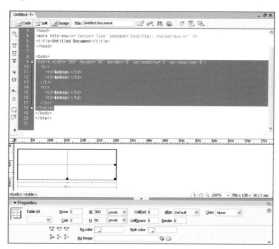

```
<table>
  <tr>
    <td> </td>
  </tr>
</table>
```

Table HTML format

Tables have general properties and cell properties. General properties are inserted between HTML <table> tags and are applied to the whole table, while cell properties are inserted between <tr> or <td> tags and control the properties of each cell.

Inserting a Table

There are two ways to insert a table into a Web page: through the Menu bar or the Insert bar.

To insert a table using the Menu bar, move the mouse cursor to the position you want to insert the table and select Insert > Table from the Menu bar. This method is not used often because it is less convenient than using the Insert bar.

The Insert bar method is used more often because you can insert a table with just a few mouse clicks. Simply select Common > Table from the Insert bar at the top of the Dreamweaver window.

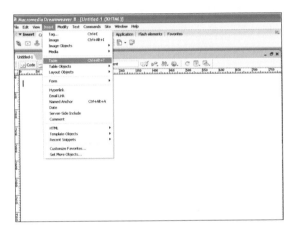 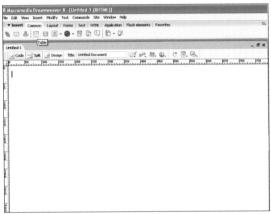

The Table dialog box offers the following options.

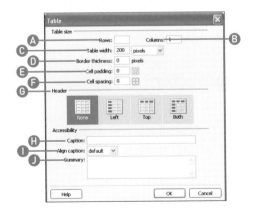

Ⓐ **Rows**: Allows you to select the number of rows for your table. This corresponds to the <tr> tag in HTML.

Ⓑ **Columns**: Allows you to select the number of columns for your table. This corresponds to the <td> tag in HTML.

Ⓒ **Table width**: Allows you to define the width of your table.

Ⓓ **Border thickness**: Allows you to define the thickness of your table border.

Ⓔ **Cell padding**: Allows you to set the spacing within each cell in your table (that is, the distance between a cell border and the object within the cell).

ⓕ Cell spacing: Allows you to set the amount of space between cells.

ⓖ Header: Allows you to select the cell into which a title is inserted. This generates the <th> tag rather than the <td> tag. This also applies center alignment and the <b> tag (for bold text) to the text in this cell.

ⓗ Caption: Allows you to give a title to the table. Only one caption may be given for each table.

ⓘ Align caption: Allows you to set the alignment of the caption.

ⓙ Summary: Allows you to insert a description of the table.

```
<table>
  <caption align="top">
    title
  </caption>
  <tr>
    <td></td>
  </tr>
</table>
```

Caption tag

Table and Cell Settings

To use tables properly, you must understand the properties of tables and cells. When you select a table and open the Properties inspector, it becomes the Table Properties inspector. It becomes the Cell Properties inspector when you select a cell within a table.

The Table Properties Inspector

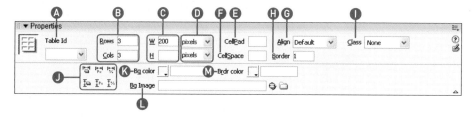

ⓐ Table Id: Allows you to specify a table name.

ⓑ Rows/Cols: Allows you to change the number of rows and columns in a table.

ⓒ W/H: Allows you to set the width and height of a table. Two units can be used: pixels or % (percent).

ⓓ Pixels/Percent: Allows you to set the width and height of a table in pixels or percent values.

ⓔ CellPad: Allows you to set the space between the content of a cell and the cell border.

ⓕ CellSpace: Allows you to set the spacing between cells.

G Align: Allows you to select an alignment method for a table.

H Border: Allows you to set the border thickness of a table. The default value is 1.

I Class: Applies the selected CSS to a table.

J Clear Column Widths/Clear Row Height: Removes unnecessary space from cells. If a table contains only blank cells, this option will reduce the total width and height by decreasing the vertical and horizontal space within cells.

K Bg color: Allows you to select a background color.

L Bg Image: Allows you to select a background image.

M Brdr color: Allows you to select a border color.

The Cell Properties Inspector

To change the settings for any cell in a table, first select the cell that you want to change. After selecting a cell, you can change its options in the Cell Properties inspector. To select a cell in the table, just move the mouse cursor to that cell by clicking your mouse in the cell.

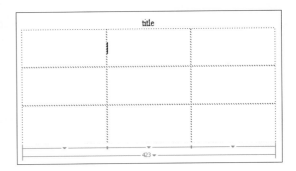

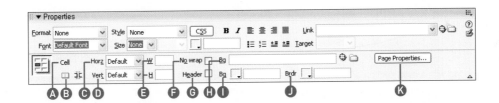

A Merge selected cells using spans: Allows you to select two or more consecutive cells while pressing Shift and then merge them.

B Split cell into rows or columns: Allows you to split a selected cell into two or more rows or columns.

C Horz: Allows you to align objects in a cell horizontally.

D Vert: Allows you to align objects in a cell vertically.

E W/H: Allows you to set the width and height of the selected cell.

F No wrap: Prevents auto linefeed when a lengthy piece of text is inserted in a cell.

G Header: Adds the <th> tag in HTML. The text in the selected cell is displayed in bold and center-aligned.

H Bg image: Allows you to select a background image for the cell.

I Bg color: Allows you to select a background color for the cell.

61

J Brdr: Allows you to select a border color for the cell.

K Page Properties: Allows you to select page properties.

Table and Cell Selection

You can select tables and cells in Code view or Design view.

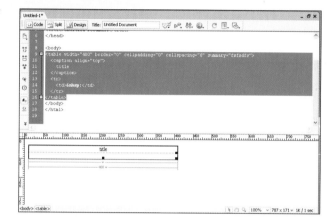

Selecting Tables and Cells in Code View

In Code view, select the corresponding HTML tags for tables and cells as you would in a word-processing program.

tip >>

When working with a long section of HTML code, such as that for a table, it is convenient to use the new source code collapsing feature of Dreamweaver 8. This allows you to compartmentalize sections of code so that you can take an overall view of your HTML.

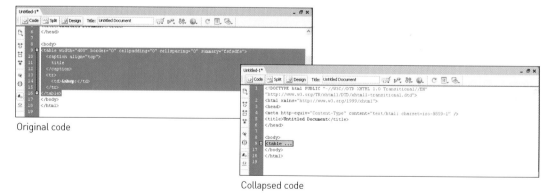

Original code

Collapsed code

Click the "-" icon (next to Line Numbers) in Code view to collapse the source code to one line. Click it again to expand the source code.

Selecting Tables and Cells in Design View

Another method for table selection is to click on the table while in Design view. In this case you should take care not to change the table size when selecting the table with your mouse. A handy method for avoiding this potential problem is to drag with your mouse from a blank space over part of the table.

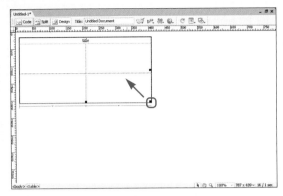

You can also select a table with your keyboard. First, move the mouse cursor to the right of the table. Then, while pressing the Shift key, press the left arrow key to select the table. Similarly, you can move the mouse cursor to the left of the table and press the Shift key and the right arrow key.

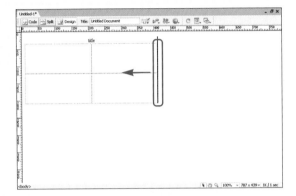

Selecting cells is just as easy. Click a desired cell to select it, then move to another cell using the arrow keys. When the mouse cursor moves to another cell, that cell is selected.

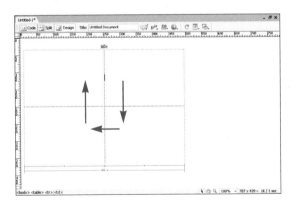

One of the most frequently used methods for selecting a cell is to click in the Tag Selector (above the Properties inspector). This allows you to select the cell's HTML tag.

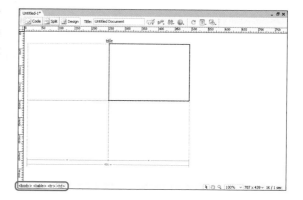

You can select multiple adjacent cells simply by clicking and dragging with your mouse. Alternatively, hold down the Shift key as you click each individual cell.

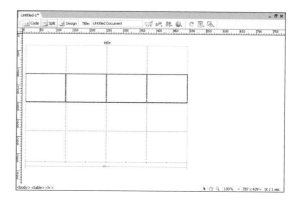

Select multiple non-adjacent cells by holding the Ctrl key as you click them.

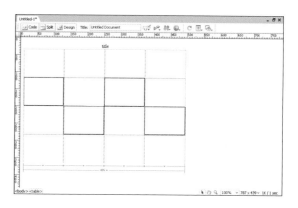

1

Using Tables to Create a Faux Message Board

A table can be used to define the overall layout of a Web page, align objects, or act as content itself. In this exercise, we'll create a table to act as a message board, which is one of the most basic types of content that can be inserted into a Web page.

Start File
\Sample\03_file\board_page.htm

Final File
\Sample\03_file\board_page_end.htm

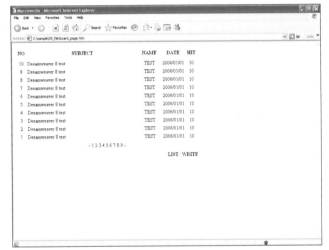

Final page

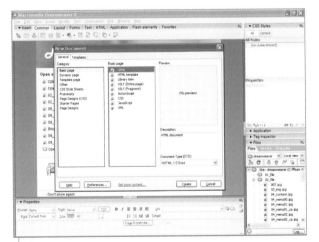
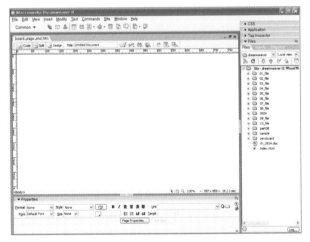

1 Select File > New from the Menu bar to open a new page. It is important to save when you first open a new page, before proceeding. Here we will save it as board_page.htm.

65

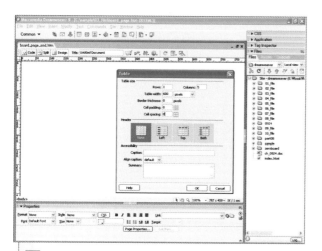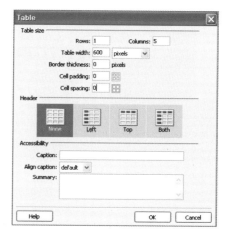

2   First, we will create a table to be used as a title. Select Common > Table from the Insert bar. When the Table dialog box appears, enter 1 for Rows, 5 for Columns, 600 pixels for Table width, 0 for Border thickness, 0 for Cell padding, and 0 for Cell spacing. Then click OK.

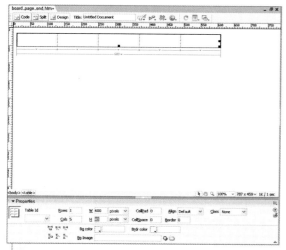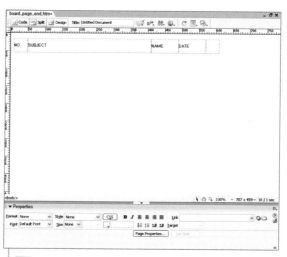

3   Select the table and set the table height to 40.

4   Specify the properties of the table cells from left to right, as shown below.

Cell	Width	Content
First Cell	40	NO
Second Cell	360	SUBJECT
Third Cell	80	NAME
Fourth Cell	80	DATE
Fifth Cell	40	HIT

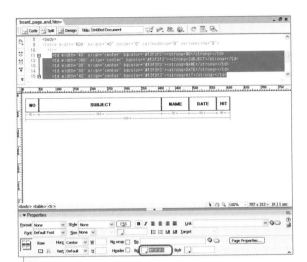

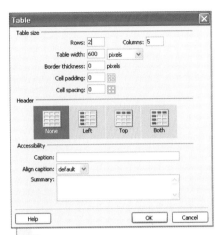

5 Select all the cells with your mouse and choose Align to Center so that all text is center-aligned. In the Properties inspector, click the Bold icon and set the cell background color to #F3F3F3.

6 To insert a new table, move the mouse cursor to the right of the first table and select Common > Table from the Insert bar. When the Table dialog box appears, enter 2 for Rows, 5 for Columns, 600 pixels for Table width, 0 for Border thickness, 0 for Cell padding, and 0 for Cell spacing. Then click the OK button.

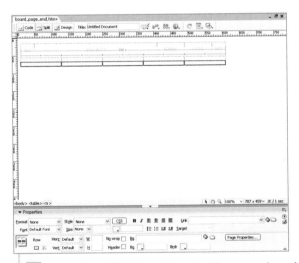

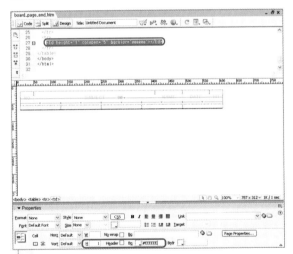

7 When the table is inserted, select the second row by dragging with your mouse. Then click the Merge selected cells using spans icon in the Properties inspector to merge the cells.

8 Set the background color of the merged cell to #EEEEEE and its height to 1. Then click the Split button and delete the " ;" that was inserted into the cell in Code view. In this way you allow a long line at the bottom of the table.

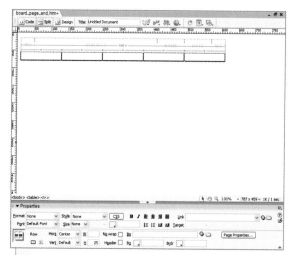

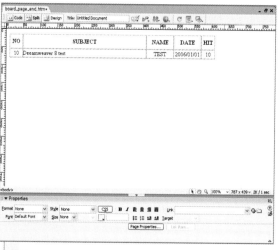

9 Select all the cells in the second row of the second table with your mouse. Set their height to 25, then choose Align to Center. For the second cell in the row, however, select Left alignment, which is the default setting.

10 Enter the width value and content of each cell as shown below.

Cell	Width	Content
First Cell	40	10
Second Cell	360	Dreamweaver 8 test
Third Cell	80	TEST
Fourth Cell	80	2006/01/01
Fifth Cell	40	10

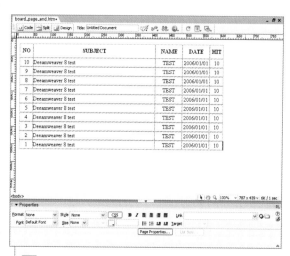

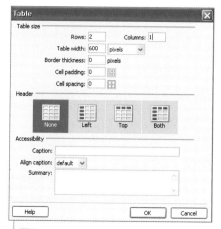

11 Select the row you just entered values for and copy it to make 10 rows, as shown here. Then change the NO column value of the 10 rows to 10 through 1, beginning from the top.

12 Move the mouse cursor to the right of the last row and select Common > Table from the Insert bar. When the Table dialog box appears, enter 2 for Rows, 1 for Columns, 600 pixels for Table width, 0 for Border thickness, 0 for Cell padding, and 0 for Cell spacing. Then click the OK button.

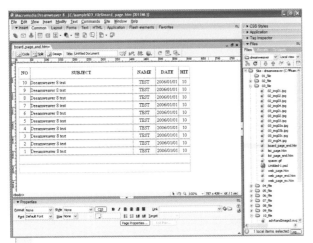

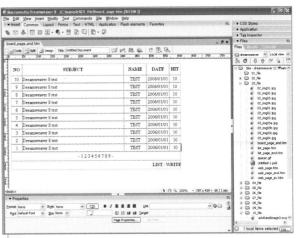

13 Select the new table and set the table height to 60. Set the alignment to Center for the first row, and Right for the second row.

14 Select the first row and enter "- 1 2 3 4 5 6 7 8 9 -". Then enter "LIST / WRITE" in the second row.

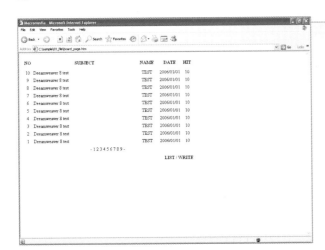

15 Save the edited document. Then click F12 to preview it in a Web browser.

tip >>

Cell Sizing

A table's cells are automatically sized based on the number of cells in the table and the table's overall height and width parameters. Of course, specifying height and/or width for an individual cell will alter the auto-sizing of the remaining cells. For example, if the width of the table is 300 pixels and there are three cells in a row, the width of each cell is set to 100 pixels. If the width of one cell has been defined as 150 pixels, the width of the other two cells is automatically set to 75 pixels each.

Exercise

2 Using Ghost Images to Correct Cell Spacing

When producing a "shopping mall" Web page, it is essential to effectively arrange and display the images, descriptions, and prices for many products. To insert a variety of content in a single page, as in the following example, you can use a table to position and arrange that content. In this case, we will use "ghost" or transparent images to create a balanced table.

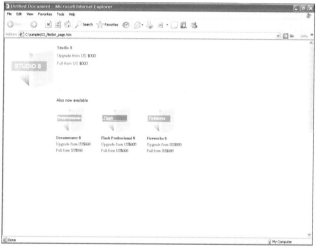

Final page

Start File
\Sample\03_file\list_page.htm

Final File
\Sample\03_file\list_page_end.htm

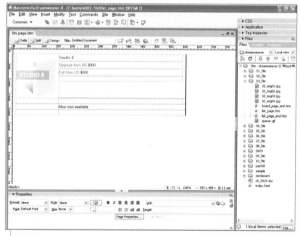

1 Open the \Sample\03_file\list_page.htm file in Dreamweaver.

2 All the files that are to be inserted into the table can be found in the \Sample\03_file folder in the File panel. In past versions of Dreamweaver, images were inserted using the Select Image Source dialog box. You can now drag images from the File panel directly to the desired table cell.

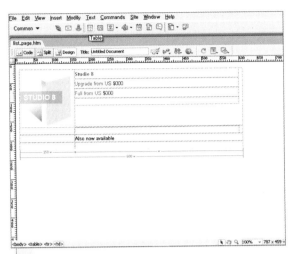

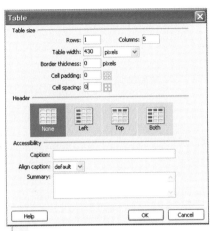

3 Move the mouse cursor to the last cell and select Common > Table from the Insert bar.

4 When the Table dialog box appears, enter 1 for Rows, 5 for Columns, 430 pixels for Table width, 0 for Border thickness, 0 for Cell padding, and 0 for Cell spacing. Then click the OK button. This table is for the layout for product list 1. Here we will call it "Product List 1."

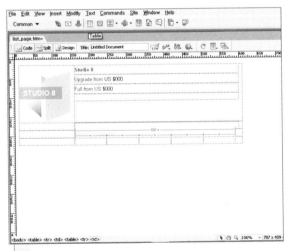

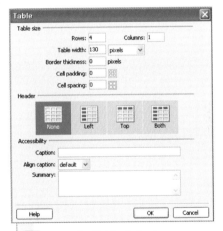

5 When the Product List 1 table is created, move the mouse cursor to the first cell and select Common > Table from the Insert bar.

6 When the Table dialog box appears, enter 4 for Rows, 1 for Columns, 130 pixels for Table width, 0 for Border thickness, 0 for Cell padding, and 0 for Cell spacing. Then click the OK button. This table is for the layout of product list 2. Here we will call it "Product List 2."

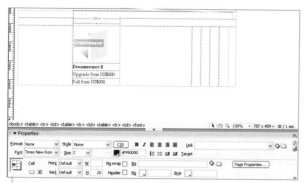

7 Insert images and text in the first cell of Product List 2, as shown here. Select a text color as you wish. Set the height of the text cells to 20 pixels.

8 Select a cell of the Product List 2 table and set its width to 130 pixels.

note >>>

Step 7 Cell Contents

- Image: \Sample\03_file\02_img02.jpg

- Text: Enter "Dreamweaver 8" in the second cell, "Upgrade from US $000" in the third cell, and "Full from US $000" in the fourth cell.

tip >>

Using Ghost image

When you set the table width as a percentage (%), or when there is an empty cell into which no object is inserted, the table shape may be distorted when you display the page in a Web browser. When an empty cell is the culprit, you can insert a ghost image (basically, a small, invisible graphic) into the cell to prevent such distortion.

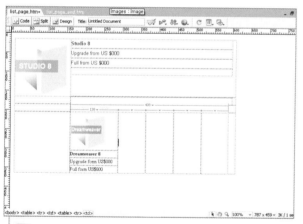

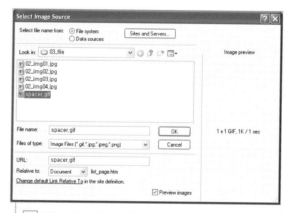

9 Next, we will insert a ghost image in the second cell of the Product List 1 table to ensure proper table spacing. Move the mouse cursor to the second cell and select Common > Image from the Insert bar.

10 When the Select Image Source dialog box appears, select the file spacer.gif and click the OK button.

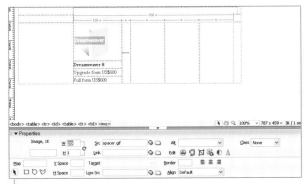

11 Once the mouse cursor is in the second cell, press Shift and the ← key at the same time to select a ghost image. When the ghost image is selected, set the image width to 20 pixels in the Properties inspector.

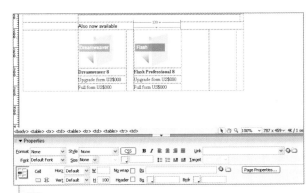

12 Copy the Product List 2 table to the third cell of the Product List 1 table.

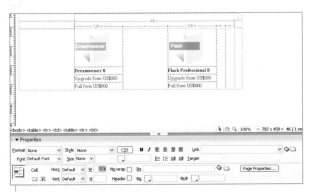

13 Enter the content for the newly copied table, as described below. We will call this table "Product List 3." Select the first cell of Product List 3, insert the product image, and set the cell width to 130 pixels.

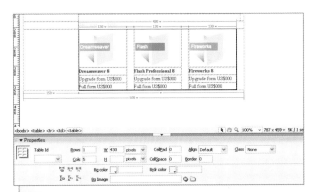

14 In the same manner described previously, insert a ghost image in the fourth cell of the Product List 1 table, and copy the Product List 3 table to the fifth cell of product List 1 to create the Product List 4 table. Then change the content to the image and text described below.

---

note >>>

Step 13 Cell Contents

- Image: \Sample\03_file\02_img03.jpg
- Text: Enter "Flash Professional 8" in the second cell, "Upgrade from US $000" in the third cell, and "Full from US $000" in the fourth cell.

note >>>

Step 14 Cell Contents

- Image: \Sample\03_file\02_img04.jpg
- Text: Enter "Fireworks 8" in the second cell, "Upgrade from US $000" in the third cell, and "Full from US $000" in the fourth cell.

15 Save the edited document. Press F12 to preview it in a Web browser.

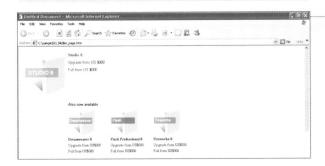

Creating a Ghost Image

A ghost image is also called a blank image. It refers to a transparent image 1 pixel in size. Ghost images are used in many ways when producing Web pages. The most frequently used application is to create a blank space of a fixed size in a Web page layout or table. Typically, you will use a graphic program such as Photoshop to create a ghost image; it must be created in GIF or PNG format, as these support transparency.

Creating A Ghost Image in Photoshop

In this section, we will learn how to create a ghost image in Photoshop (in this example, version CS).

01 Start Photoshop. Press Ctrl-N. When the New dialog box appears, open a work window with a size of 1 pixel on each side.

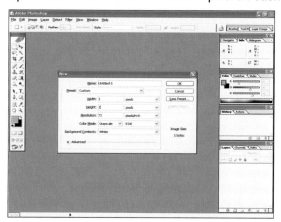

02 Create a new layer and delete the Background layer to make the work window transparent.

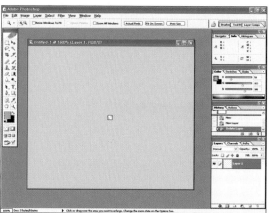

03 Select File > Save for Web from the Menu bar. When the Save for Web dialog box appears, save the file in GIF format.

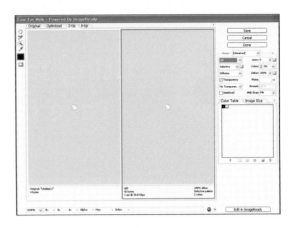

Creating A Ghost Image in Dreamweaver

You can also create a ghost image in Dreamweaver.

01 Start Dreamweaver and select Edit > Preferences from the Menu bar.

02 When the Preferences dialog box appears, click the Layout Mode category.

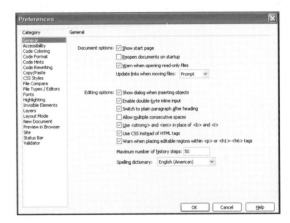

03 Click the Create button to the right of "Image file."

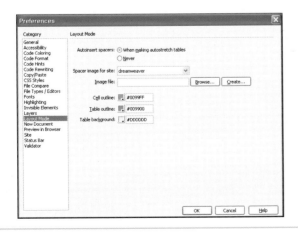

04 When the Save Spacer Image File As dialog box appears, you can see that the spacer.gif filename is automatically set. Select a folder to save the file to.

3

Using Tables to Create a Page Layout

The following exercise requires that you create, arrange, and manage several tables to create a page layout. In order to insert and conveniently manage multiple tables on one page, you can use the code collapsing feature in Code view.

Source Folder
\Sample\03_file\

Saved File
\Sample\03_file\web_page_ex.htm

Final File
\Sample\03_file\web_page_end.htm

Final pages

Creating Tables

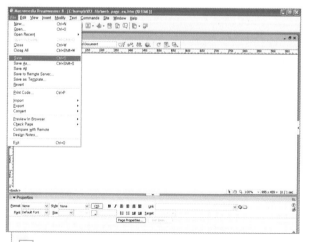

1 Start Dreamweaver and create a new document. Select File > Save from the Menu bar to save the file. Here we will save it as \Sample\03_file\web_page_ex.htm.

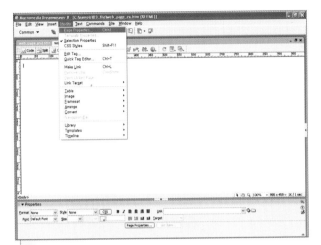

2 First, define page properties. Select Modify > Page Properties from the Menu bar.

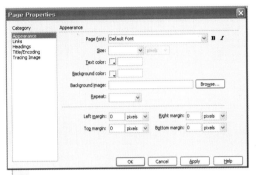

3 When the Page Properties dialog box appears, enter 0 for all the margin values in the Appearance category. Click the OK button.

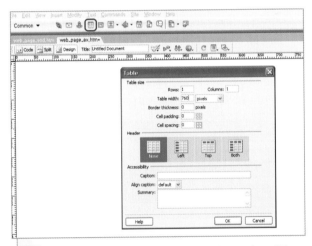

4 Select Common > Table from the Insert bar. When the Table dialog box appears, enter 1 for Rows, 1 for Columns, 760 pixels for Table width, 0 for Border thickness, 0 for Cell padding, and 0 for Cell spacing. Then click the OK button. We will call this table "Table 1."

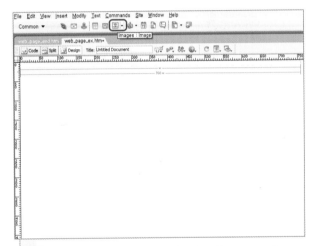

5 Select a cell of Table 1 and select Common > Image from the Insert bar.

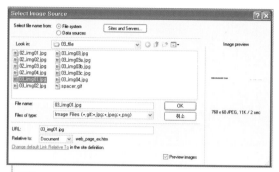

6 When the Select Image Source dialog box appears, select the file 03_img01.jpg and click the OK button.

7 Click in a blank space under the table in the work window. Move the mouse cursor to the right of the table. To create a new table, select Common > Table from the Insert bar. When the Table dialog box appears, enter 1 for Rows, 2 for Columns, 100 percent for Table width, 0 for Border thickness, 0 for Cell padding, and 0 for Cell spacing. Then click the OK button. We will call this table "Table 2."

8 Select the first cell of Table 2 and set its width to 760 pixels, but do not set the width value of the second cell.

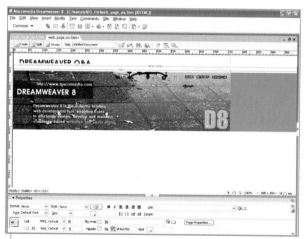

9 Select Common > Image from the Insert bar to insert the image \Sample\03_file\03_img02.jpg into the first cell of Table 2. For the second cell, set the background color to #4687B6.

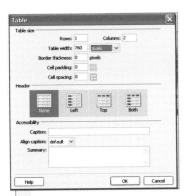

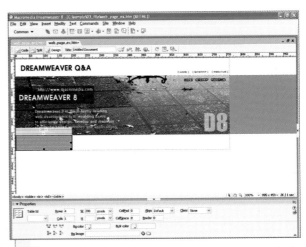

10 Below Table 2, create a new table with 1 for Rows, 2 for Columns, 760 pixels for Table width, 0 for Border thickness, 0 for Cell padding, and 0 for Cell spacing. We will call this table "Table 3."

11 Set the width of the first cell of Table 3 to 200 pixels and its background color to #4687B6. Then create a new table with 4 for Rows, 1 for Columns, 200 pixels for Table width, 0 for Border thickness, 0 for Cell padding, and 0 for Cell spacing. We will call this "Table 4."

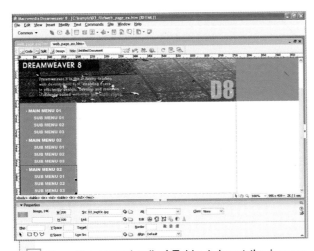

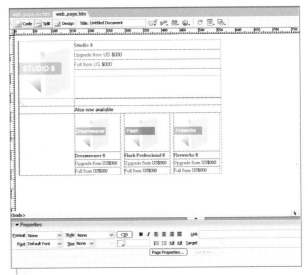

12 From the second cell of Table 4, insert the images sequentially, as shown below.

13 Open the source code file, \Sample\03_file\web_page.htm.

note >>>

Step 12 Source Files

\Sample\03_file\03_img03a.jpg

\Sample\03_file\03_img03b.jpg

\Sample\03_file\03_img03c.jpg

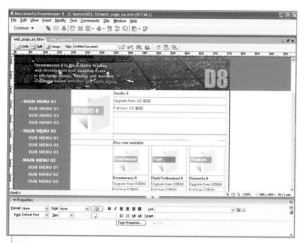

14 Copy the contents of the web_page.htm file and paste it in the right cell of Table 3.

15 Save the edited document. Then click F12 to preview it in a Web browser.

Managing Code in Each Table Using Code Collapsing

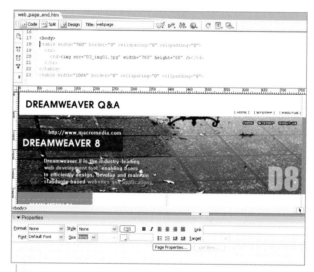

1 Now let's arrange the source code using the HTML code collapsing feature. First, click the Split button to see Code view and Design view at the same time.

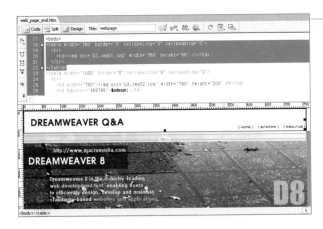

2 To collapse the source code of Table 1, first select it in Design view. You can see that the source code for the table is set as a block and connected by the symbol ▣.

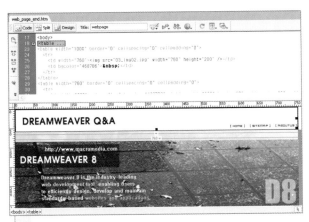

3 Click the symbol ▣ with your mouse. It changes to the ⊞ symbol, and the source code block collapses to one line.

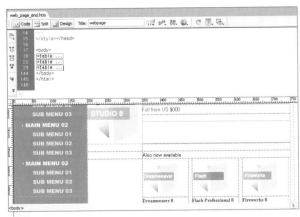

4 In the same manner described above, collapse the source code of the other tables. You can see that the HTML code has been considerably reduced.

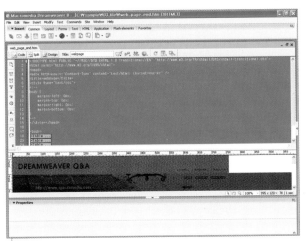

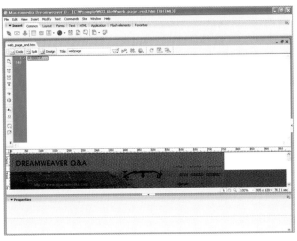

5 Likewise, you can use the collapsing feature to collapse similar tags. In the example above, all the tags have been collapsed into one by clicking the + symbol.

Chapter | 4

Using Layers to Create Visual Effects

Layers provide an excellent means for exerting total control over your page layouts. They also allow for dynamic visual designs that may challenge your notions of the Web's limitations. In this chapter, we'll introduce the finer points of using layers in Dreamweaver, then jump into some exercises that demonstrate why layers are so crucial to Web design.

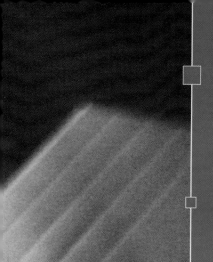

An Introduction to Layers

S ince layers can be critical when designing advanced Web pages, it's fortunate that Dreamweaver makes them so easy to implement. In this section we'll cover the basics before moving on to the exercises.

What Is a Layer?

When you insert objects such as text, images, and tables into an HTML document, they are positioned at the top left of the page by default. To arrange them, you alter their alignments or you use tables. These methods position elements relative to one another within HTML documents. Layers, on the other hand, use absolute position values so you can place elements in any position you want. Before setting absolute position values, add the desired objects to a layer.

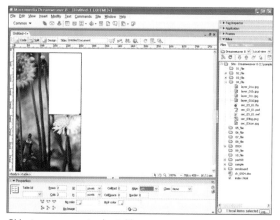

Object arrangement using tables

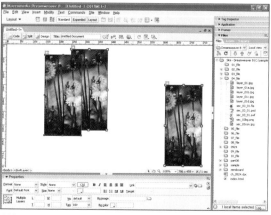

Object arrangement using layers

Changing the Stacking Order

One unique characteristic of layers is that you can overlap them. When overlapping layers, the stacking order of the layers has an impact on the display of each layer. You can change the stacking order of layers by changing their z-index values in the Layers panel or the Properties inspector; a higher value translates to a higher position in the stack.

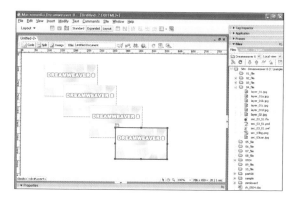

84

Creating and Configuring Layers

You can create layers using the Insert bar or with HTML tags. Dreamweaver also lets you create layers automatically using CSSs.

Creating a Layer Using the Insert Bar

To insert a layer, select Layout > Draw Layer from the Insert bar. Then, in Design view, click-and-drag the layer with your mouse.

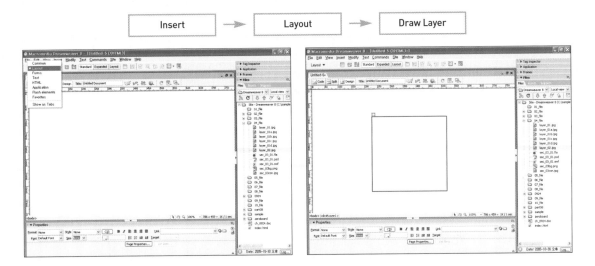

Creating Layer Code Using HTML Tags

As shown here, you can also create a layer using HTML code, but this is a much more complicated way of doing things.

```html
<html>
<head><title></title>
<script language="JavaScript" type="text/JavaScript">
<!
function MM_reloadPage(init) {  //reloads the window if Nav4 resized
  if (init==true) with (navigator) {if ((appName=="Netscape")&&(parseInt(appVersion)==4))
{
    document.MM_pgW=innerWidth; document.MM_pgH=innerHeight; onresize=MM_reloadPage; }}
    else  if  (innerWidth!=document.MM_pgW  ||  innerHeight!=document.MM_pgH)
location.reload();
}
MM_reloadPage(true);
//   >
</script>
</head>
<body>
<div id="Layer1" style="position:absolute; left:141px; top:37px; width:230px;
height:221px; z  index:1"></div>
</body>
</html>
```

Creating Layers Using CSSs

As shown in this example, you can also create a layer using cascading style sheets, which allow for greater detail than HTML.

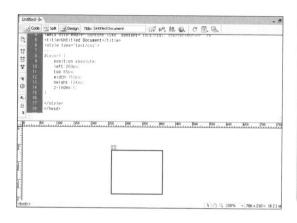

```
<html >
<head><title></title>
<style type="text/css">
<!
#Layer1 {
        position:absolute;
        left:117px;
        top:32px;
        width:110px;
        height:118px;
        z  index:1;
}
    >
</style>
</head>
<body>
<div id="Layer1"></div>
</body>
</html>
```

Moving and Resizing Layers

You can move a layer with your mouse or resize it using the resize handles.

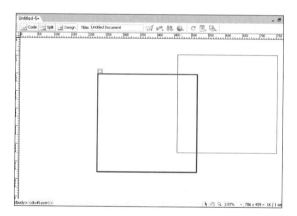

Layers have more resize handles than images. Images are positioned in the upper left of a page, so you can resize them using the three resize handles at the upper-right and bottom corners. Since layers are positioned by absolute values, you can resize them in any direction using eight resize handles.

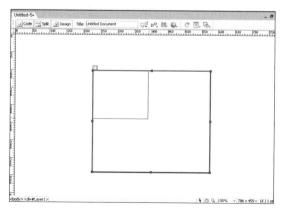

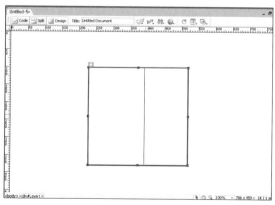

The Layers Panel

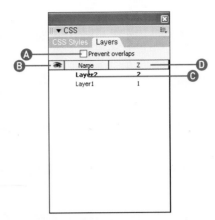

Ⓐ Prevent overlaps: You can choose whether or not to allow layers to overlap. If the box is unchecked, overlapping will be allowed.

Ⓑ Visibility (👁): Determines how layers are displayed in a Web browser. Make a selection for each layer.

Default: Defers to the default values of the Web browser.

Inherit: Inherits the properties of the parent layer.

Visible: Always shows the layer.

Hidden: Hides the layer from the page.

Ⓒ Name: Allows you to specify a name for each layer.

Ⓓ Z: Allows you to decide the stacking order of layers. A higher value translates to a higher position in the stack.

The Layer Properties Inspector

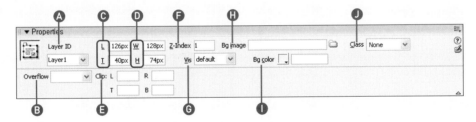

Ⓐ Layer ID: Allows you to specify a name for the selected layer. The layer name must be different from those of tables and images.

Ⓑ Overflow: When image or text content is larger than the layer, there are four options for how content will be displayed: visible, hidden, scroll, and auto.

Visible: This is the default setting. The layer becomes larger to show all contents.

Hidden: The part of the content that is outside the layer is hidden.

Scroll: Horizontal and vertical scroll bars are displayed, with the layer becoming larger if necessary.

Auto: Automatically activates scroll depending on the content of the layer. In other words, if the content is larger than the layer, the scroll bars are activated.

C **L/T**: Specifies the coordinates of the layer. By default, the top-left corner of a Web browser window has the coordinates 0,0.

D **W/H**: Sets the width and height of the layer. As with tables, even an object that is larger than the layer can be inserted into the layer.

E **Clip**: Allows you to select the areas you want to show on the Web page regardless of the layer size. There are four options: L (left), R (right), T (top), and B (bottom).

F **Z-Index**: Allows you to decide the stacking order of layers. When layers overlap, layers with higher z-index values are placed above layers with lower values.

G **Vis**: Defines the visibility of the layer. By default, the visibility property is not specified.

Default: Defers to the default values of the Web browser.

Inherit: Inherits the properties of the parent layer.

Visible: Always shows the layer.

Hidden: Hides the layer from the page.

H **Bg image**: Allows you to select a background image for the layer.

I **Bg color**: Allows you to select a background color. If you don't enter a value, the layer becomes transparent.

J **Class**: Allows you to apply a CSS to the layer.

1

Laying Out a Page with Layers

Unlike other objects inserted into an HTML document, layers can be positioned by absolute values. Moreover, they can be easily resized or repositioned using your mouse. This is more convenient than arranging objects with tables. However, as there are some restrictions to layers, you should understand how to accurately apply layer properties. In this exercise, we will learn how to lay out a page with layers.

Source Folder
\Sample\04_file\

Start File
\Sample\04_file\layer_page.htm

Final File
\Sample\04_file\layer_page_end.htm

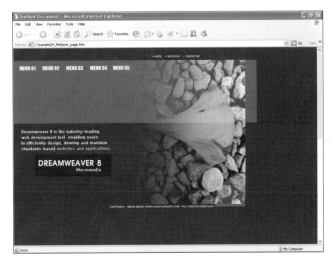

Final page

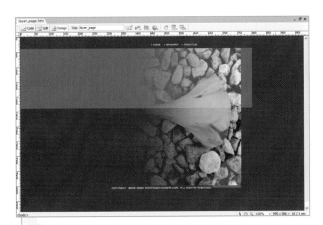

1 Open the file \sample\04_file\ layer_page.htm.

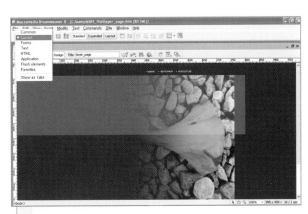

2 Select Layout > Draw Layer from the Insert bar.

89

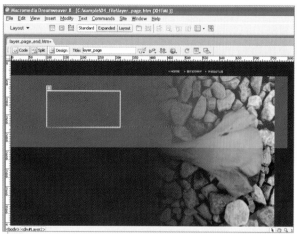

3 In Design view, use your mouse to draw a layer as shown here. You don't have to accurately specify the layer size. We will call this layer "Layer 1."

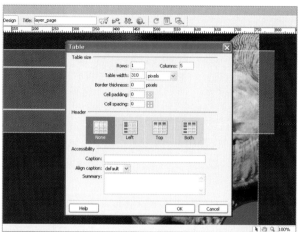

4 Select Layer 1 with the mouse. Select Layout > Table from the Insert bar. When the Table dialog box appears, enter 1 for Rows, 5 for Columns, 310 pixels for Table width, 0 for Border thickness, 0 for Cell padding, and 0 for Cell spacing. Then click the OK button.

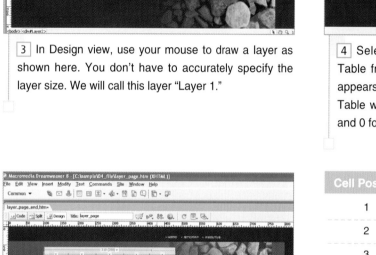

5 We'll now insert images into the table cells. Using Common > Image, add images to each cell according to the table on the right.

Cell Position	Path
1	C:\sample\04_file\layer_page_01.jpg
2	C:\sample\04_file\layer_page_02.jpg
3	C:\sample\04_file\layer_page_03.jpg
4	C:\sample\04_file\layer_page_04.jpg
5	C:\sample\04_file\layer_page_05.jpg

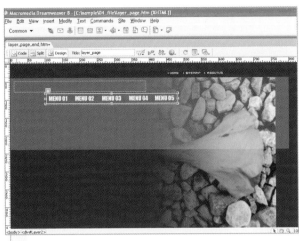

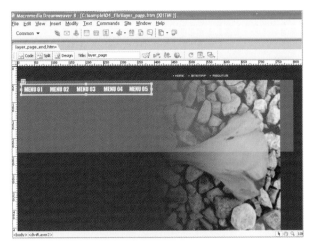

6 Move Layer 1 as shown here. Then resize it using the resize handles so that it fits into the table you created in step 4.

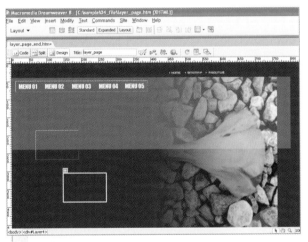

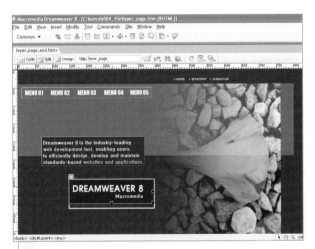

7 Select Layout > Draw Layer from the Insert bar to insert a layer, then click the Draw Layer button again to insert another layer. We will call these two layers "Layer 2" and "Layer 3."

8 Select each of the layers and insert the images shown below.

note >>>

Step 8 Images

Layer 2: \Sample\04_file\layer_page_11.jpg

Layer 3: \Sample\04_file\layer_page_12.jpg

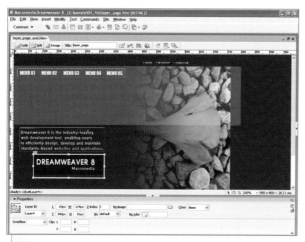

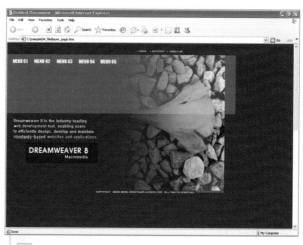

9 Move Layer 2 and Layer 3 as shown here. To move them, you can use the arrow keys on your keyboard or directly enter the L, T, W, and H values in the Properties inspector.

10 Save the edited document. Click F12 to preview it in a Web browser.

Inserting a Flash Banner Using a Layer

Layers can be used to freely position or arrange objects such as text, images, and tables. In this exercise, we will insert a Flash element into a layer to position and arrange it on a Web page.

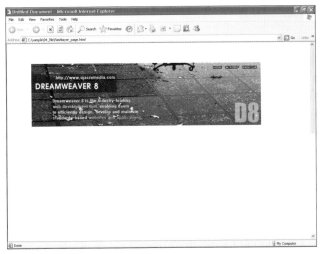

Final page

1 Select File > New from the Menu bar to create a new document. Save this document as flashlayer_page_ex.htm by selecting File > Save.

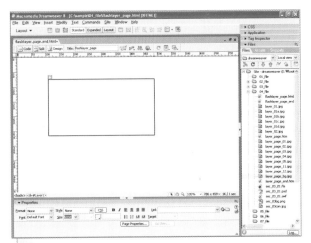

2 Select Layout > Draw Layer from the Insert bar to draw a layer.

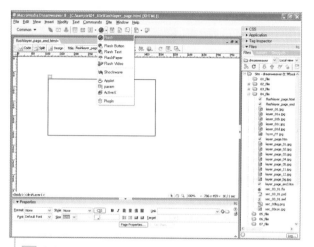

3 Select the layer and select Common > Flash from the Insert bar.

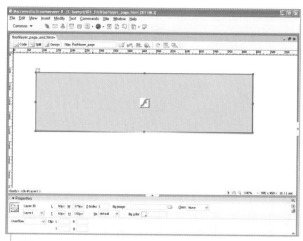

4 When the Select File dialog box appears, select the file sample\04_file\sec_03_01.swf. Then click the OK button.

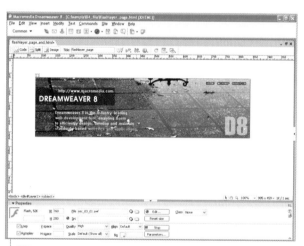

5 Select the Flash element and click the Play button in the Properties inspector to preview it. You can move the layer in which the Flash element has been inserted to the desired position.

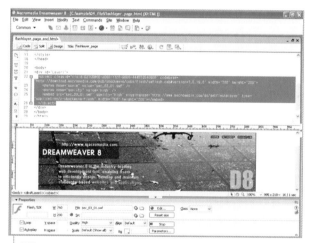

6 Click the Split button to see the Code and Design views at the same time. Usually you would use many lines of source code to insert a Flash element in Dreamweaver. However, we can do this with basic code only.

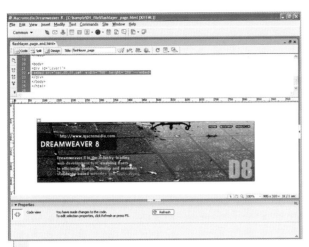

7 We will reduce the source code for the Flash element, as shown below.

8 Save the edited document and click F12 to preview it in a Web browser.

[Before change]

```
<object classid="clsid:D27CDB6E   AE6D   11cf   96B8   444553540000" codebase="http://download.
macromedia.com/pub/shockwave/cabs/flash/swflash.cab#version=7,0,19,0" width="760" height="200">
    <param name="movie" value="sec_03_01.swf" />
    <param name="quality" value="high" />
                               <embed        src="sec_03_01.swf"        quality="high"
pluginspage="http://www.macromedia.com/go/getflashplayer" type="application/x  shockwave  flash"
width="760" height="200"></embed>
  </object>
```

[After change]

```
<embed src="sec_03_01.swf"  width="760" height="200"></embed>
```

Chapter | 5

Frames

Web sites that manage dozens to hundreds of Web pages, containing massive amounts of information, often use the HTML technique called frames. Frames are used for many applications, such as navigation of Web pages and repetition of data on multiple pages of a Web site. Even empty (blank) frames can be useful in creating a Web site. This chapter describes the concepts and uses of frames.

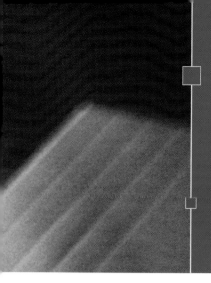

Understanding Frames

With the rapid growth of the Internet, the volume of Web site content is increasing dramatically. It is not an easy thing to put so much diverse content into one Web site. Efficient management of a large volume of information is an endless issue for site administrators. There are many alternatives and solutions to this problem, and one of them is the production and management of a Web site that uses frames.

Frames and Framesets

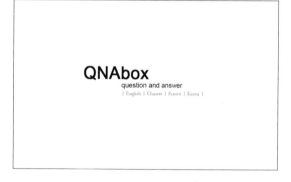

The example above is a Web site with a lot of content in many languages. This site makes it all available through a single Web site address using frames.

Frames provide a method for integrating many HTML documents into one document. For example, if a layout is to be composed of three areas, you can define these areas as frames and then insert a separate HTML document into each frame. An additional HTML document, called a frameset, is then required to ensure that the other HTML documents are "talking to each other."

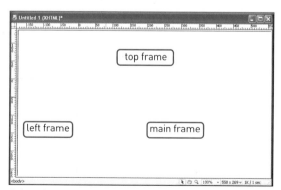

A three-frame page layout

A frameset consists of the following HTML tags:
```
<frameset rows="130,*" cols="*" >
  <frame src="frame1.htm" name="topFrame" >
  <frameset rows="*" cols="170,*" >
        <frame  src="frame2.htm" name="leftFrame" >
        <frame  src="frame3.htm  " name="mainFrame" >
  </frameset>
</frameset>
```

The corresponding HTML

To insert a frame into a page, select Layout > Frames from the Insert bar.

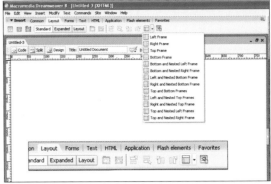

Inserting a frame from the Insert bar

Alternatively, you can insert a predefined frame configuration by selecting Create from Sample > Framesets from the Menu.

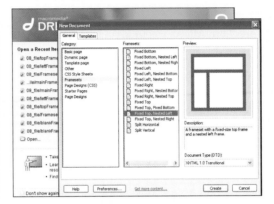

Selecting a predefined frame layout

The Frame Properties Inspector

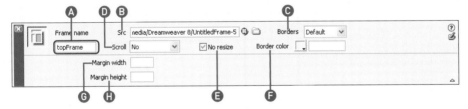

Ⓐ **Frame name**: Allows you to use the frame name as the target name (essentially, you can select the frame name for HTML linking purposes).

Ⓑ **Src**: Allows you to define the path of the HTML document used for the frame.

Ⓒ **Borders**: Allows you to activate borders for the frame.

Ⓓ **Scroll**: Allows you to activate scrolling within the frame.

Ⓔ **No resize**: Allows you to prevent visitors from resizing frames in their Web browsers.

Ⓕ **Border color**: Allows you to set the border color.

Ⓖ **Margin width**: Allows you to set the inner-margin width of the frame document.

Ⓗ **Margin height**: Allows you to set the inner-margin height of the frame document.

The Frameset Properties Inspector

Dreamweaver also allows you to create framesets automatically and edit them using the Properties inspector.

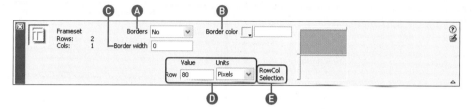

Ⓐ **Borders**: Allows you to set the border between frames.

Ⓑ **Border color**: Allows you to set the border color.

Ⓒ **Border width**: Allows you to set the border width.

Ⓓ **Row**: Allows you to select each frame in the frameset.

Ⓔ **RowCol selection**: Allows you to select each frame in the frameset.

Linking Pages to Frames

To produce a Web site using frames, you must link HTML pages to their corresponding frames. In addition to the basic target settings—_blank, _parent, _self, and _top—Dreamweaver automatically adds frame names to the available choices in the target selection list. In other words, when you assign a target (that is, a destination for a given link/HTML document) you can select a frame by name, as opposed to a pop-up window, for instance.

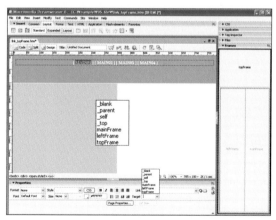

Selecting frames from the target selection list

100

Using Blank Frames

While frames are often used to create user interfaces, they can also be used for other specialized purposes. For example, blank frames are used in many Web sites. As the name suggests, a blank frame is a frame that has no content. To set this up, the HTML document is created with two frames; the size of one frame is set to 0 to hide it and the actual contents are inserted into the other frame. In this way, even if the user moves between different pages, all the pages are displayed in one frame in the frameset. The benefit of this is that the same address is displayed even when different pages are displayed. As can be seen in the sample images below, even if you enter a subpage, the URL in the address window does not change.

Main page of Web site

Subpage of Web site

iframe

Often used to insert a message board or visitor's book into a page, iframe is a technique for creating a defined space on a page and loading another page into that space. You can think of it as a single, floating frame. You can insert an iframe in Dreamweaver 8 by using the <iframe>, </iframe> tags in Code view, as shown below.

Inserting a bulletin board with iframe

iframe

```
<html>
<head><title>Untitled Document</title>
</head>
<body><div align="center">
<iframe src="http://www.dreamweaverqna
.com/zeroboard/zboard.php?id=frame_board0
1" frameborder="1" width="600" height=
"300" ></iframe>
</div>
</body>
</html>
```

Even though iframe can easily load other pages to a separate space, it does have problems related to the creation of multiple scroll bars. If your content will fit inside a given iframe, no scroll bar will be generated. However, if you place an object larger than the size specified by iframe, multiple scroll bars may be generated on one page. As the sample image demonstrates, this is hardly a desirable effect!

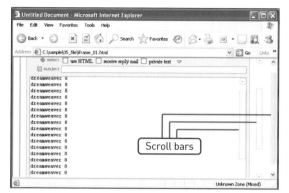

Three scroll bars on one page

Include

Include is another variation of the frame concept. The difference in this case is that you can load multiple HTML documents into a single space. To an extent you can think of this as frames within frames.

When a Web programmer and designer work together with one frame, they often use Include. The Include method is similar to using frames, but scroll bars do not appear. The Include syntax is used in HTML to give a visual effect and for production and management convenience. Because it requires knowledge of server script languages (ASP and PHP format), this method is not used often for Web sites that are created by Web designers alone. However, Web designers can use this method easily if they understand the simple syntax.

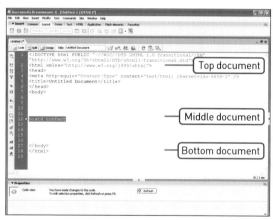

Include

Inserting Include

Include can be inserted directly into code within Code view or from the Insert bar. When you insert Include using the Insert bar, it changes depending on the format of the inserted file.

To insert Include from the Insert bar, you generally select HTML > Script and use SSI; this is the method used to insert HTML documents. However, documents written in a server script languages such as ASP, PHP, or JSP can also be inserted using Include. Note that the tools in the Insert bar vary a little depending on the language of the inserted document.

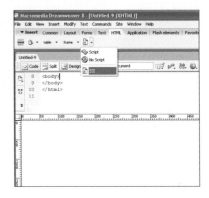

Inserting an HTML Document

Select HTML > Script > SSI from the Insert bar.

Inserting an ASP Document

Select ASP > Include from the Insert bar.

Inserting a PHP Document

Select PHP > Include from the Insert bar.

Inserting a JSP Document

Select JSP > Include Directive from the Insert bar.

Creating Frames and Framesets

Dreamweaver allows you to click a predefined frameset to instantly configure a page, or to create and add frames individually as needed. In this example, we will create and save multiple frames and an additional frameset—all HTML documents—using the Layout menu in Dreamweaver.

Final Files

\Sample\05_file\topFrame_edit.htm, leftFrame_edit.htm, mainFrame_edit.htm, Frameset_edit.htm

Final page

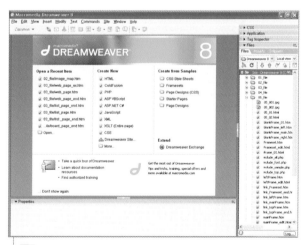

[1] From the Create New sub-menu of the Dreamweaver Start window, select HTML to create a new HTML document.

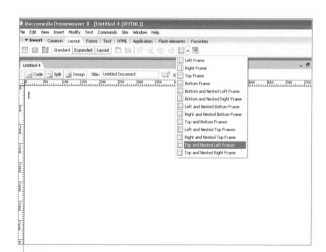

[2] Click the Layout > Frames button from the Insert bar and then click Top and Nested Left Frames. This is generally called the frameset for L-shaped layout. The top frame has the default name "topFrame," the bottom-left frame, "leftFrame," and the bottom-right frame, "mainFrame."

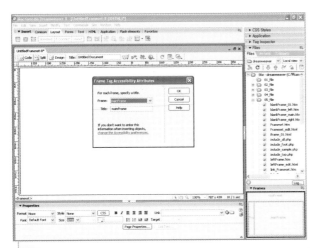

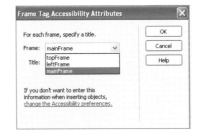

3 | As shown in the figure, enter a frame name and title in the Frame Tag Accessibility Attributes dialog box, and click the OK button.

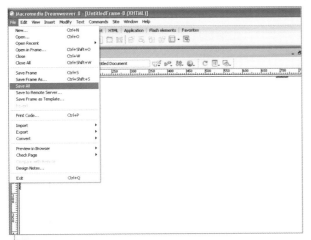

4 | Select File > Save All from the Menu bar. Make sure that frameset is selected in the Frames panel before saving.

5 | When the Save As dialog box appears, enter "Frameset.htm".

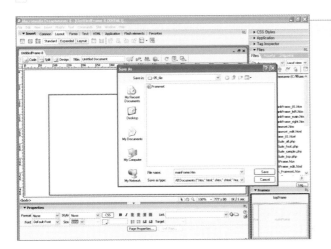

6 | Now we'll save each frame document. With mainFrame selected in Design view, save the document as mainFrame.htm in the Save As dialog box. Using the techniques described in this exercise, you can use frames to construct virtually any page layout.

When you select framesets and frames, Dreamweaver indicates an active selection with a heavy line.

When saving framesets, it's important to accurately name the frames, as these names are automatically assigned as paths to the frames.

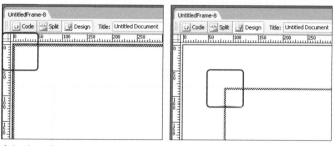

Selecting a frameset   Selecting a frame

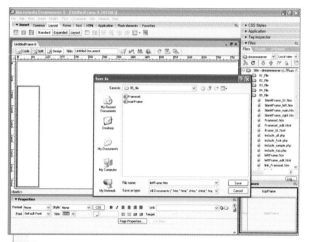

7   With leftFrame selected, save as leftFrame.htm.

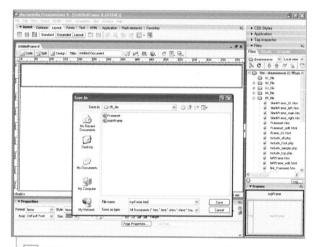

8   With topFrame selected, save as topFrame.htm.

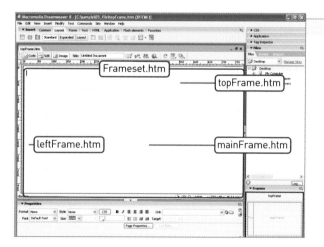

9   You can see that the four files—topFrame.htm, leftFrame.htm, mainFrame.htm, and Frameset.htm— have been saved to form one page. Using the techniques described in this exercise, you can use frames to construct virtually any page layout.

Setting Frame and Frameset Properties

You can set properties such as size, name, and background color for frames and framesets using the Properties inspector. In this exercise, we will modify the properties of the frames and frameset saved in the previous exercise.

Start Files

\Sample\05_file\topFrame.htm, leftFrame.htm, mainFrame.htm, Frameset.htm

Final Files

\Sample\05_file\topFrame_edit.htm, leftFrame_edit.htm, mainFrame_edit.htm, Frameset_edit.htm

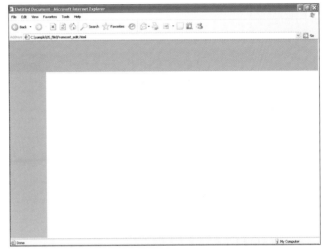

Final page

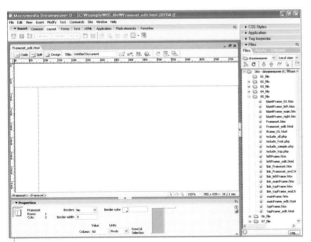

1 Open the file \Sample\ 05_file\Frameset.htm.

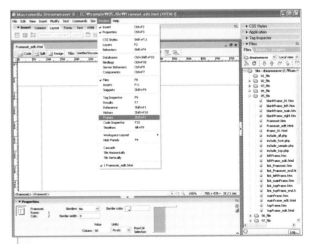

2 You can see that the frames are set. Select Window > Frames from the Menu bar.

The Frames panel is used to select specific frames and framesets with a mouse click.

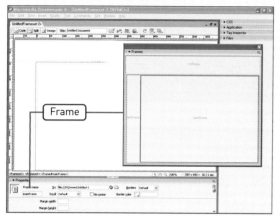

Selecting a frameset

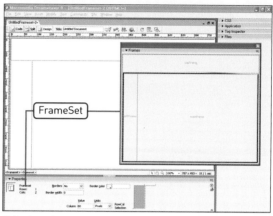

Selecting a frame

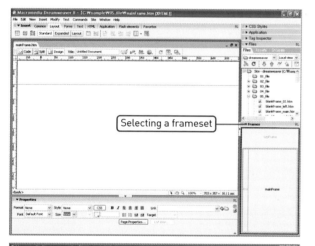

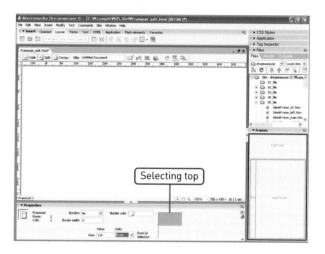

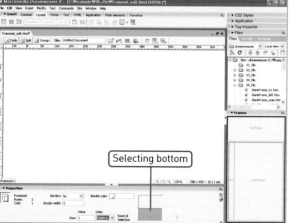

Select the top of RowCol Selection	Select the bottom of RowCol Selection
Borders: No	Borders: No
Border Color: None	Border Color: None
Border Width: 0	Border Width: 0
Row Column: 100, Pixels	Row Colunn: 1, Relative

3   When the Frames panel opens, select and modify the frames in the Properties inspector as shown here.

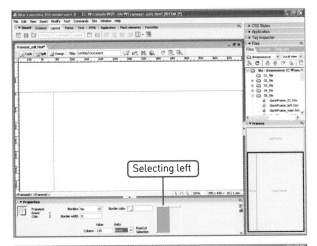

Selecting left

Select the left of RowCol Selection	Select the right of RowCol Selection
Borders: No	Borders: No
Border Color: None	Border Color: None
Border Width: 0	Border Width: 0
Row Column: 100, 166Pixels	Row Colunn: 1, Relative

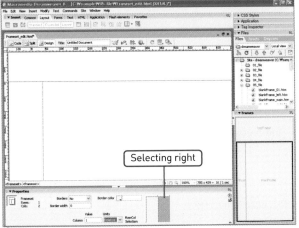

Selecting right

4 Select the frameset at the bottom of the Frames panel and modify the properties in the Properties inspector as shown here.

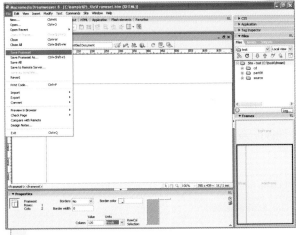

5 Select File > Save Frameset from the Menu bar to save the edited frameset document.

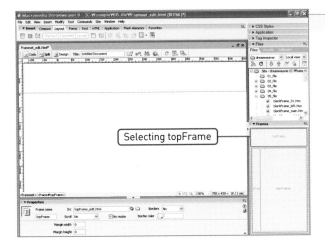

Selecting topFrame

6 We have modified the properties of the frameset. Now we will modify the properties of each frame. Click topFrame in the Frames panel. We will change the background color in the Properties inspector as shown below.

Frame name: topFrame (used as target name)
Src: topFrame.htm
Borders: No
Scroll: No
No resize: Checked
Margin width: 0
Margin height: 0

Before configuring an individual frame, you should always select the No resize option. If you create a Web site without setting the No resize option, users can move the frame border by dragging it. In other words, users could arbitrarily change the Web site layout.

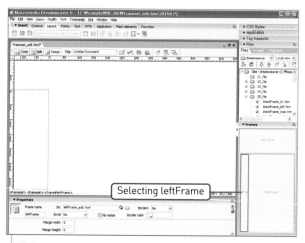

Selecting leftFrame

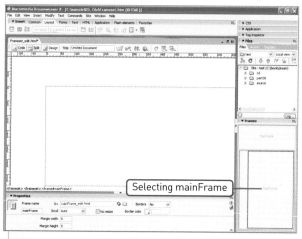

Selecting mainFrame

[7] Select leftFrame in the Frames panel and change the properties as shown below.

[8] Select mainFrame in the Frames panel and change the properties as shown below.

Frame name: leftFrame (use as target name)	Frame name: mainFrame (use as target name)
Src: leftFrame.htm	Src: mainFrame.htm
Borders: No	Borders: No
Scroll: No	Scroll: Auto
No resize: Checked	No resize: Checked
Margin width: 0	Margin width: 0
Margin height: 0	Margin height: 0

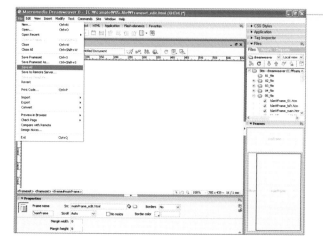

[9] Select File > Save All from the Menu bar to save all the modified documents.

Saving Frames

Save Frame, Save Frameset, or Save All are generally used to save an edited frame or frameset. You can select File > Save Frame from the Menu bar (if a frame is selected) or select File > Save Frameset from the Menu bar (if a frameset is selected).

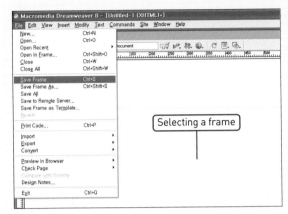

Selecting a frame

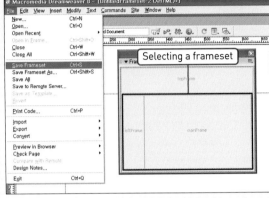

Selecting a frameset

Frames with the same background color

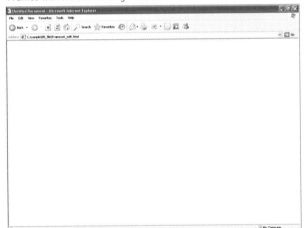

Frames with different background colors

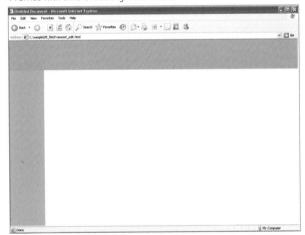

10 Save the edited documents and press the F12 key to preview them. Since the pages have no properties, the frames cannot be differentiated. However, if you specify a different background color for each page, you can differentiate the frames. The exercise is now complete.

Exercise

3

Producing a Web Site Using Frames

To produce a Web site using frames, you must link pages to each frame properly. If the links are incorrect, incorrect pages may be visible to Web site visitors. Before you link a page to a frame, the frame should have a name. In this exercise, we will define a frame name for each frame and set links with the frame names as targets.

Source Files

\Sample\05_file\link_topFrame. htm, link_leftFrame.htm, link_main Frame.htm, link_Frameset.htm, 05_01.htm

Final Files

\Sample\05_file\link_Frameset_ end.htm, link_topFrame_end.htm

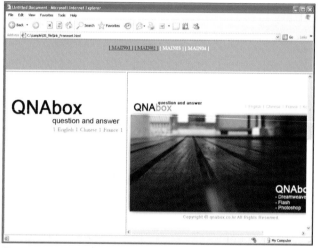

Final page

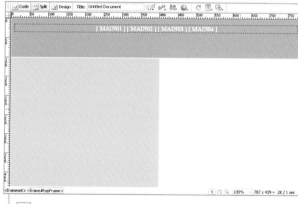

1 Open the file \Sample\05_file \link_Frameset.htm.

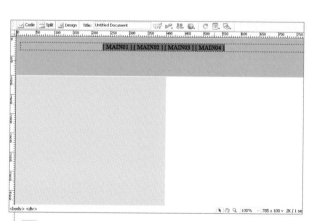

2 You can see that the document consists of three frames. We will define a link to the text of topFrame.

tip >>

To divide a frame with the mouse, first set the frame border to Visible and then drag the frame border with the mouse.

❶ Select View > Visual Aids > Frame Borders from the Menu bar.

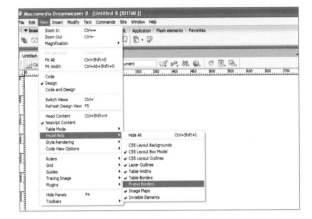

❷ Drag the frame border from left to right with the mouse, as shown.

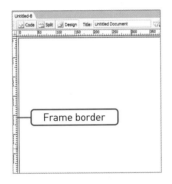

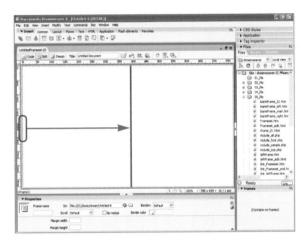

❸ Drag the frame border from top to bottom to create an additional row of table cells. Drag from top to bottom with the Ctrl key held down to create a row of merged cells.

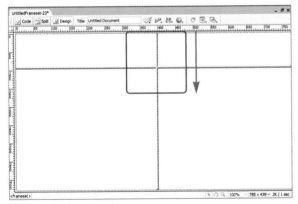

Dragging the frame border

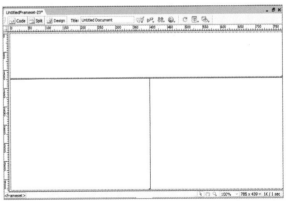

Dragging while holding down Ctrl

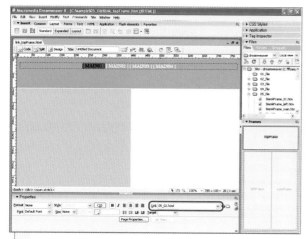

3 Select MAIN01 and enter "05_02.html" in the Link section of the Properties inspector.

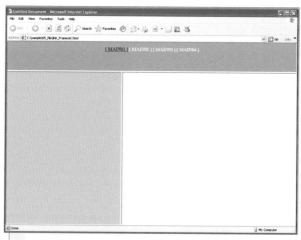

4 Press F12 to preview it. You can see that MAIN01 of topFrame is linked as shown in the figure.

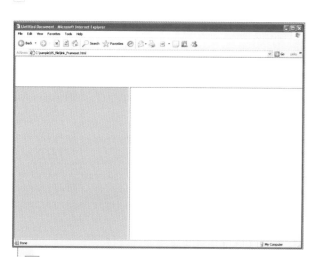

5 Click MAIN01. You can see that the linked site (\sample\05_file\05_02.html) opens in topFrame. This is because unless a target is separately defined, the default target is set to "_self."

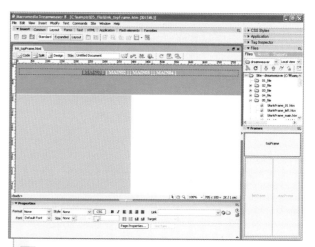

6 Close the browser and return to Dreamweaver.

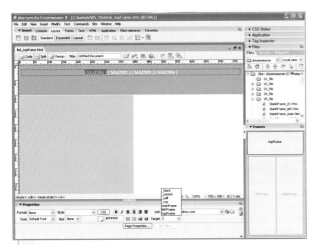

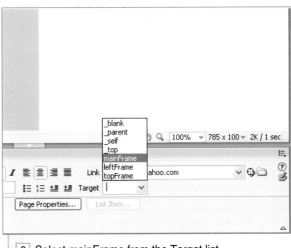

7 Click MAIN01 to select it. When you click Target in the Properties inspector, _blank, _parent, _self, _top, mainFrame, leftFrame, and topFrame appear.

8 Select mainFrame from the Target list.

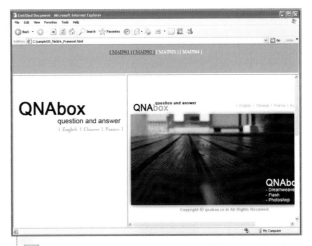

9 Press F12 to preview it. When you click MAIN01 of topFrame, the linked site opens in mainFrame.

10 Now link the URL "\sample\05_file\05_01.htm" to MAIN02 of topFrame and set its target to leftFrame. You can see that there are no scroll bars in leftFrame, but there are scroll bars in mainFrame. This is because Scroll is set to No in the MAIN02 Properties inspector.

Despite the benefits of creating a Web site with framesets, this approach creates a number of problems. You need to accurately assess the size of objects inserted into an HTML document to fit within the frame size. You also need to set the frame border so that it cannot be dragged by visitors, or else the Web site layout may be changed unexpectedly by the Web site producer or administrator. The figures below show examples of working configurations.

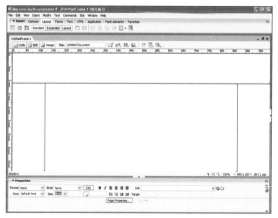 

Examples of properly configured frames

Another problem is automatic registration by search sites whose search engines surf Web sites and register them using meta tag keywords. The issue is that these search engines do not register framesets, only the frames that make them up.

Lastly, it is not easy to print Web site content created with framesets. If you try to print such a Web site, only one frame of the frameset will be printed. You will have to select the frame you want in the print settings. For this reason, some sites provide a separate printable page.

 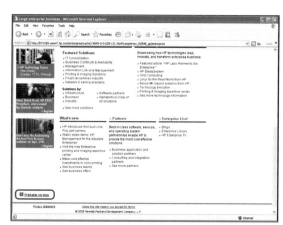

Original page   Printable version

There are two main methods for creating blank frames: to hide a frame completely or to make a frame appear not to exist by making it identical to the background. In this example, we will create a frame that has dimensions but is identical to the background.

Start Files

\Sample\05_file\blankFrame_01. htm, blankFrame_left.htm, blankFrame_right.htm, blankFrame_main.htm

Final Files

\Sample\05_file\blankFrame_01_ end.htm, blankFrame_left_end. htm, blankFrame_right_end.htm, blankFrame_main_end.htm

Final page

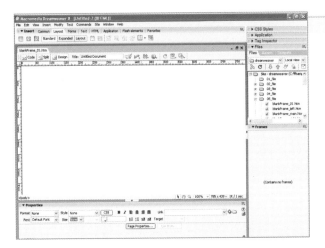

1 From the Create New sub-menu of the Dreamweaver Start window, select HTML to create a new HTML document.

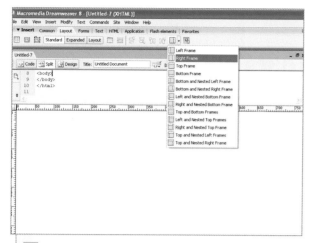

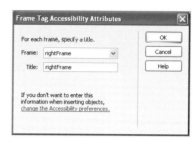

2 | Select Layout > Frame from the Insert bar and click Right Frame. When the Frame Tag Accessibility Attributes dialog box appears, check the default settings and click the OK button.

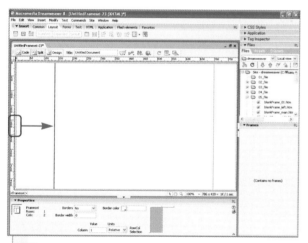

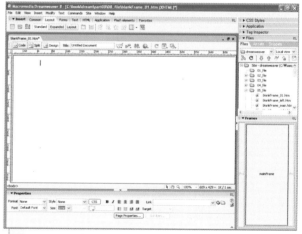

3 | Divide a frame with the mouse. Drag the left frame border from left to right as shown in the figure.

4 | You can see that there are three frames. This means that three frames comprise one page. See the sample HTML code below.

tip >>

Adding a Frame

To add a frame to an existing frame, drag the left frame border. If you drag the frame border with just the mouse, a new frame will be added to the existing frame; if you drag the frame border while holding the Ctrl key, a new frame will be created on top of the existing frame.

```
<frameset rows="*" cols="80,*,80"
framespacing="0" frameborder="no" border="0">
        <frame src="#" name="leftFrame">
        <frame src="#" name="mainFrame" >
<frame src="#" name="rightFrame°± >
</frameset>
```

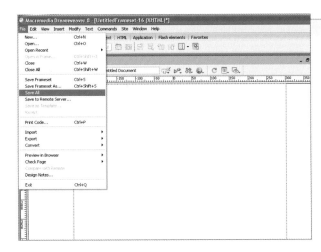

5 Select File > Save All from the Menu bar to save all the modified documents. Use the file names given below.

note >>>

Step 5 File Names

Frameset: blankFrame_01.htm

Each frame: blankFrame_left.htm, blankFrame_right.htm, blankFrame_main.htm

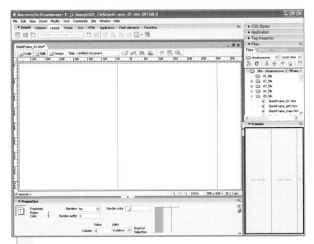

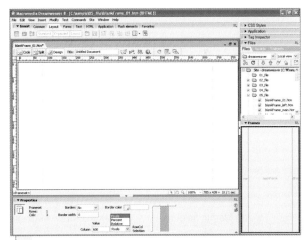

6 To specify the properties of a frameset, select the frameset in the Frames panel. Then select the left box in the RowCol Selection of the Properties inspector, 1 for Columns, and Relative for Units.

7 Next, select the middle box in the RowCol Selection of the Properties inspector, 600 for Columns, and Pixels for Units. Likewise, select the right box in the RowCol Selection of the Properties inspector, 1 for Columns, and Relative for Units. The purpose of these settings is to place the center frame at the center of the page regardless of the browser size.

Left frame

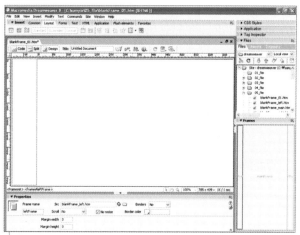

Right frame

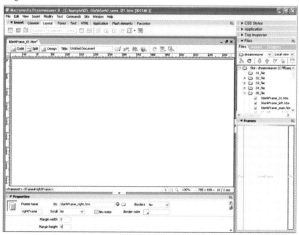

8 Now define the properties of each frame. Select the left and right frames in the Frames panel and enter the values given below.

Left frame	Right frame
Frame name: leftFrame	Frame name: rightFrame
Src: blankFrame_left.htm	Src: blankFrame_right.htm
Scroll: No	Scroll: No
No resize: Checked	No resize: Checked
Border: No	Border: No
Margin width, Margin height: 0	Margin width, Margin height: 0

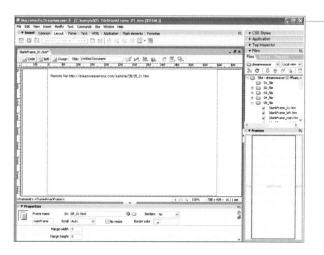

9 Select the middle frame in the Frames panel and enter the values shown below.

Frame Name: mainFrame

Src: 05_01.htm

Scroll: Auto

No Resize: Checked

Border: No

Margin Width, Margin Height: 0

Main page

Subpage

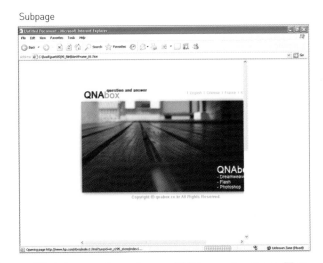

10 Select File > Save All from the Menu bar to save all the modified documents, and press F12 to preview them. Then click the menus in the previewed page to move to subpages. You can see that the URL of the page does not change even if you move to subpages. Moreover, as the link target of the site is set to "_self," the frameset layout is maintained.

Exercise

5

Working with One Frame Using Include

The Include tag is used to produce one document consisting of multiple pages. In this example, we will use Include to produce the top, content, and bottom pages as if they were one document.

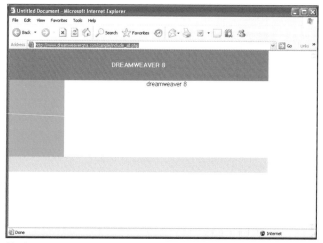

Final page

Start File
\Sample\05_file\include_sample.php

Final Files
\Sample\05_file\include_all.php, include_top.php, include_foot.php

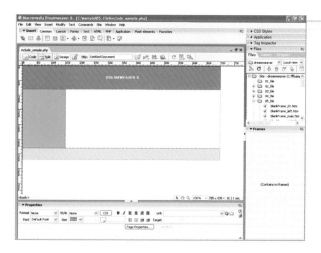

1 Open the file \Sample\ 05_file\include_sample.php.

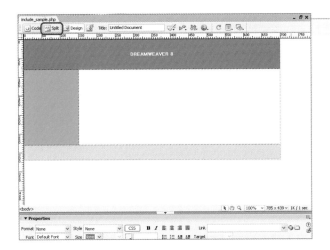

2 In order to create a Web page using the Include tag, files that are to be viewed by visitors must be saved in *.php format. Click the Split button to see Code view and Design view at the same time.

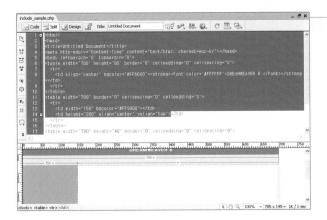

3 In Code view, select the top part (as shown at left) and copy it by pressing Ctlr-C. The copied code is shown below for reference.

```
<<html>
<head>
<title>Untitled Document</title>
<meta http  equiv="Content  Type" content="text/html; charset=euc  kr"></head>
<body leftmargin="0" topmargin="0">
<table width="700" height="80" border="0" cellpadding="0" cellspacing="0">
  <tr>
     <td  align="center"  bgcolor="#FF6600"><strong><font  color="#FFFFFF">DREAMWEAVER  8
</font></strong></td>
  </tr>
</table>
  </TR>
</TABLE>
<TABLE WIDTH="700" BORDER="0" CELLSPACING="0" CELLPADDING="0">
  <TR>
    <TD WIDTH="150" BGCOLOR="#FF9900"></TD>
    <TD HEIGHT="200" ALIGN="CENTER" VALIGN="TOP">
```

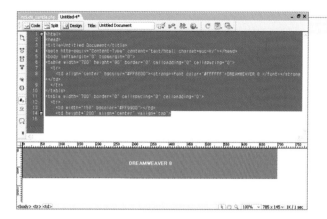

4 Select File > New from the Menu bar to open a new HTML document. Press Ctrl-A to select all the new tags. Then press Ctrl-V to replace this selection with the source code you copied in the previous step.

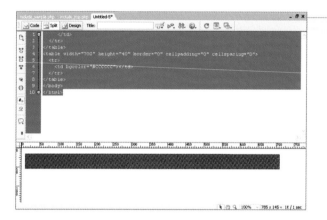

5 To save the new tags, select File > Save from the Menu bar. When the Save As dialog box appears, save it as include_top.php. Now open a new HTML document and copy the remaining code from the include_sample .php file into it. The code is shown below for reference.

```
</td>
  </tr>
</table>
<table width="700" height="40" border="0"
cellpadding="0" cellspacing="0">
  <tr>
    <td bgcolor="#CCCCCC"></td>
  </tr>
  </TR>
</TABLE>
</BODY>
</HTML>
```

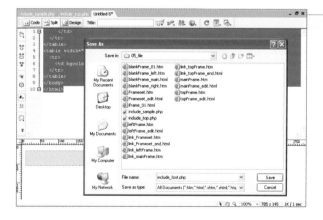

6 Save the edited document as include_foot.php. The top and bottom documents have now been completed.

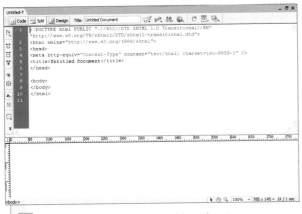

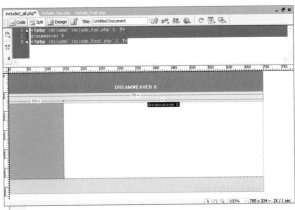

7 Select File > New from the Menu bar to open a new HTML document, and make sure that Split is selected.

8 Delete all the HTML source code in Code view and enter the code shown below. Then save the document as include_all.php.

```
<?php include('include_top.php'); ?>
dreamweaver 8
DREAMWEAVER 8
<?PHP INCLUDE('INCLUDE_FOOT.PHP'); ?>
```

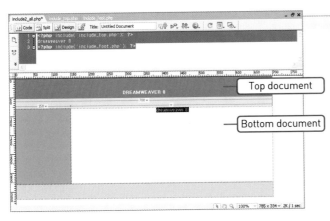

Top document

Bottom document

9 As shown in the figure, include_top.php and include_foot.php have been inserted into the Web page.

note >>>

By using the Include tag in this exercise, we were able to combine different sources of information into a single Web page. This technique can be invaluable when building complex Web sites, or when designing sites that will need to be updated by multiple administrators.

Chapter | 6

Creating Interactive Pages with Forms

To produce interactive content such as bulletin boards, member registration forms, product purchasing interfaces, and questionnaires, you need to use forms. Forms are an indispensable part of many Web pages. They allow users to send selected information to a server for processing, they communicate information that is on a server back to users, and they can even interact with Web database software. In this chapter, you will learn how to use forms in Dreamweaver and then explore what they can bring to a Web site.

Getting Comfortable with Forms

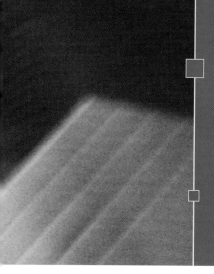

Form elements are mainly used to show or input selected information via interaction with a server or database. Form elements respond to users' behavior and have indispensable features for Web-based information delivery. In this section, we will explore and practice making form elements that play many roles.

The Basic Format of Forms

The basic HTML format for form elements is given below. There are two primary kinds of form tags: <form> and <input type>. The <form> tag determines how information will be processed. The <input type> tag determines how form data will be entered through a Web browser. In other words, the form elements that are displayed to the user are determined by the <input type> tag.

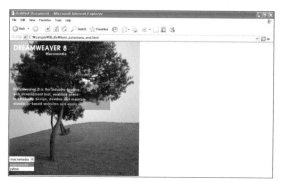

```
<form      id="form1"      name="form1"
method="post" action="">
  <input type="text" name="textfield" />
</form>
```

Inserting Form Elements

❶ To insert form elements in Dreamweaver, select Forms from the Insert bar and then the form element you want to insert.

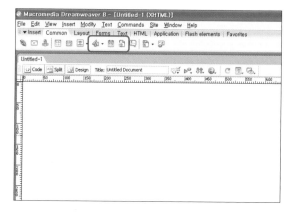

❷ You can insert each form element by clicking the corresponding form element icon. Here, we will click and insert Text Field.

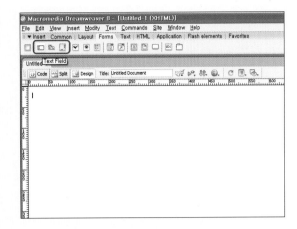

❸ Just as when inserting an image, the Input Tag Accessibility Attributes dialog box appears. To keep this dialog box from appearing automatically, select Edit > Preferences from the Menu bar. In the Preferences dialog box, uncheck Form Objects in the Accessibility category. Then click the OK button.

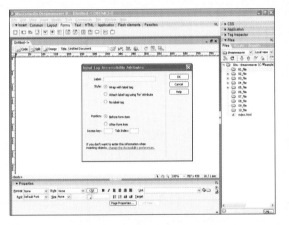 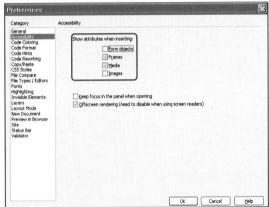

❹ When you insert a form element for the first time, a dialog box appears asking you whether to insert the <form> tag as well or only the <input type> tag. Check the Don't show me this message again checkbox and click the No button. This means that the dialog box will not open when a form tag is inserted, and you will not insert the <form> tag.

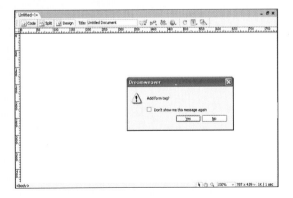

❺ If you click the Yes button to insert a form element, the <form> tag is automatically inserted also, which results in too many <form> tags in the code for one Web site. Moreover, since the <form> tag is usually inserted by Web programmers at desired positions, it is recommended that you allow the Web programmers to do this. You can see that the TextField form element has been inserted, as shown in the figure.

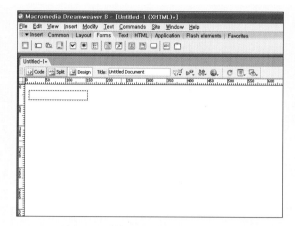

❻ When <form> and </form> tags are added in Dreamweaver, they are marked by a dotted red line in the Document window. When you select the inserted form tag, you can define their basic properties in the Properties inspector as described below.

The Form Properties Inspector

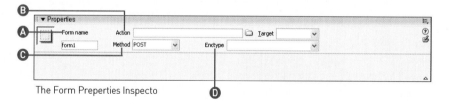

The Form Preperties Inspecto

ⓐ Form name: Allows you to specify a form name.

ⓑ Action: Allows you to designate a page that will appear when a form is submitted by a user. Examples include "login successful" and "please wait" messages.

ⓒ Method: Allows you to choose between two transmission methods: Get or Post. By choosing Get, the name of the form will be indicated in the address field of the browser when the form is sent to the server. Post will not indicate the name of the form when it's sent to the server.

ⓓ Enctype: Allows you select an encoding format. The default setting (application/x-www-form-urlencoded) is usually used with the Post method. If you are creating a file upload field, you should select the Multipart/form data format.

Form Properties

Dreamweaver enables the insertion of various form elements into Web pages. These form elements are used frequently in Web design. While form elements may be inserted and used independently, they may also act as interactive navigation elements in connection with JavaScript.

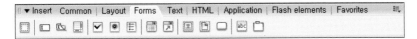

Text Field

This creates a field for inputting text. The text field may consist of one or many rows. You can also create an encrypted text field for security. When you don't input a form tag directly into the code but instead click a form element such as TextField, a dialog box appears asking you whether or not to insert form tags.

The Text Field Properties Inspector

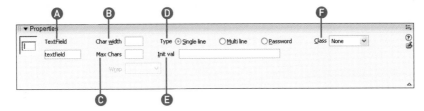

Ⓐ **TextField**: Insert a name.

Ⓑ **Char width**: Specifies the width of the field as a number of characters.

Ⓒ **Max chars**: Specifies the maximum number of characters in the field.

Ⓓ **Type**: Select Single line, Multi line, or Password.

Ⓔ **Init val**: This is text that is displayed in the field by default when the page is displayed in a Web browser.

Ⓕ **Class**: Allows you to select a style.

Hidden Field

A hidden field is used to store and send information that is input by a user. This information is not displayed to the user.

The Hidden Field Properties Inspector

Ⓐ **HiddenField**: Enter a name.

Ⓑ **Value**: Specify a value.

Text Area

A text area has the same properties as a text field and allows a user to enter multiple lines of text (as when you select Multi line for text field).

The Text Area Properties Inspector

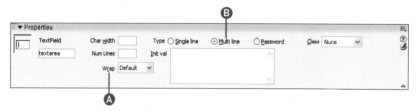

Ⓐ Wrap: Select an option for auto line feed: Default, Off, Virtual, or Physical.

Ⓑ Num Lines: Allows you to set the number of lines in the text area.

Checkbox

Checkboxes give a user the opportunity to make multiple selections from a list of options, or to clear all selections.

The Checkbox Properties Inspector

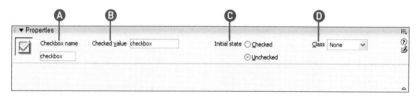

Ⓐ Checkbox name: Specify a button name for the purpose of communicating with the Web server.

Ⓑ Checked value: Input the text that will appear on the button in Web browsers.

Ⓒ Initial state: Specify an initial value (whether the boxed is checked by default when viewed in a Web browser).

Ⓓ Class: Allows you to select a style.

Radio Button

Unlike checkboxes, radio buttons allow a user to make only one selection among multiple options. Radio buttons are generally used as a group, and all the radio buttons in one group should have the same name.

The Radio Button Properties Inspector

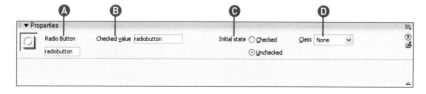

Ⓐ Radio Button: Specify a button name for the purpose of communicating with the Web server.

Ⓑ Checked value: Input the text that will appear on the button in Web browsers.

Ⓒ Initial state: Select Checked or Unchecked for the default state.

Ⓓ Class: Allows you to select a style.

Radio Group

Radio buttons can be grouped using the Radio Group form element. From the Radio Group dialog box, shown at the right, you can add or remove buttons. The invidual buttons can be separated by line breaks or laid out as a table.

List/Menu

An HTML form menu is used to allow a user to select one or more items from a list. List/Menu is appropriate for displaying many items in a narrow space and allows you to insert two types of menu: a drop-down menu from which the menu items display downward when the menu is clicked, and a scroll list menu from which an item can be selected.

The List/Menu Properties Inspector

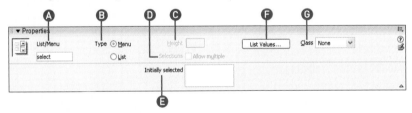

Ⓐ List/Menu: Enter a list/menu name.

Ⓑ Type: Select Menu or List. Menu shows only one item while List shows multiple items.

Ⓒ Height: Specify the height of the menu that will appear when a user selects a list menu.

Ⓓ Selections: When Allow multiple is checked, users can select multiple items from the menu.

Ⓔ Initially selected: Specifies whether any items on the list are selected by default.

Ⓕ List Values: Allows you to edit what items appear in the list.

Ⓖ Class: Allows you to select a style.

Jump Menu

You can create a jump menu using JavaScript. This is the only method that functions independently without connecting to the server.

The Insert Jump Menu Dialog Box

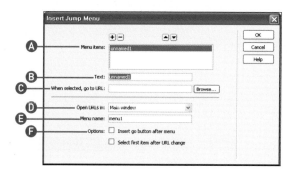 

(A) Menu items: Allows you to add menu items and change their order.

(B) Text: Enter a menu name to be displayed to the user.

(C) When selected, go to URL: Lets you enter a link address (both relative and absolute addresses are allowed) when an item is selected.

(D) Open URLs in: Specify the link target.

(E) Menu name: Enter a menu name.

(F) Options

- Insert go button after menu.
- Select first item after URL change.

Image Field

The Image Field form element allows you to use graphic files as button icons. This is a great way to make your pages more visually dynamic. To improve usability, you can even assign explanatory text to a button that will display in the browser when users mouse over it.

The Image Field Properties Inspector

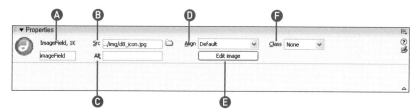

(A) ImageField: Specify an imageField name.

(B) Src: Select the location of the image.

(C) Alt: Text entered in the Alt field will be displayed in the browser when users mouse over the button.

(D) Align: Select an alignment method for images.

(E) Edit image: Open the image in an external image-editing program.

(F) Class: Allows you to select a style.

File Field

When you create a file upload field, users can select and upload any type of file from their computer. A file field is similar to a text field but it has a Browse button. Users can directly enter the path of the file to upload or search for the file by using the Browse button.

The File Field Properties Inspector

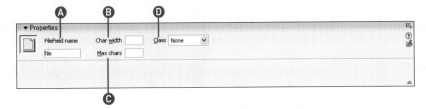

Ⓐ FileField name: Enter a FileField name.

Ⓑ Char width: Specify the length of the field for entering image file names.

Ⓒ Max chars: Specify the maximum number of characters.

Ⓓ Class: Allows you to select a style.

Button

Buttons control the jobs that can be performed by a form. Buttons are used to send data from the form to a server or to reset the form. The most frequently used labels for standard form buttons are Send, Reset, and Submit. You can also allocate other processing jobs defined by scripts. For instance, you can calculate the total number of selected items based on the values allocated to form buttons.

The Button Properties Inspector

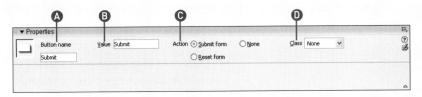

Ⓐ Button name: Specify a button name for the purpose of communicating with the Web server.

Ⓑ Value: Input the text that will appear on the button in Web browsers.

Ⓒ Action: Select a button action: Submit form, Reset form, or None.

Ⓓ Class: Allows you to select a style.

Building Site Navigation with a Jump Menu

A jump menu allows you to define many links within a small space. It is similar to the list/menu format except that the list/menu format offers only selections while the jump menu offers the option of moving between pages.

Start File

\Sample\06_file\form_jumpmenu.htm

Final File

\Sample\06_file\form_jumpmenu_end.htm

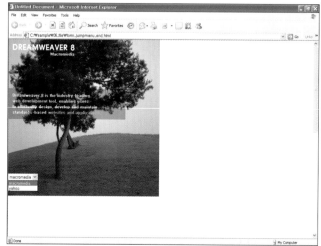

Final page

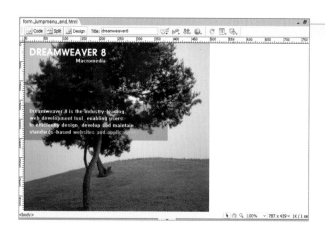

1 Select File > Open from the Menu bar to open the file form_jumpmenu.htm. You can see that the document consists of five images. The last image was designed to be inserted as a background image in such a manner that other objects can be inserted into the cell.

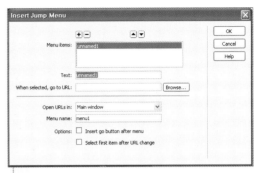

2 | Move the mouse cursor into the bottom cell and select Forms > Jump Menu from the Insert bar.

3 | The Insert Jump Menu dialog box appears.

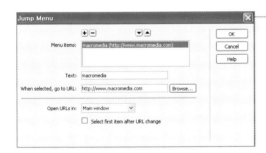

4 | In the Insert Jump Menu dialog box, enter "macromedia" in Text and "http://www.macromedia.com" in When selected go to URL. Then click the + button.

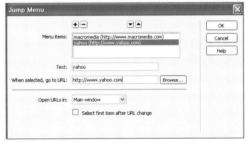

5 | To insert another menu choice, enter "yahoo" in Text and "http://www.yahoo.com" in When selected go to URL. Then click the OK button.

Let's review the HTML source code for a jump menu.

```html
<html>
<head>
<meta http equiv="Content  Type" content="text/html; charset=iso  8859  1">
<title>dreamweaver8</title>
<script type="text/JavaScript">
<!
function MM_jumpMenu(targ,selObj,restore){ //v3.0
  eval(targ+".location='"+selObj.options[selObj.selectedIndex].value+"'");
  if (restore) selObj.selectedIndex=0;
}
//    >
</script>
</head>

<body leftmargin="0" topmargin="0" marginwidth="0" marginheight="0">
<table width="500" border="0" cellspacing="0" cellpadding="0">
  <tr>
    <td height="100"><img src="form_jump01.jpg" width="500" height="100"></td>
  </tr>
  <tr>
    <td height="100"><img src="form_jump02.jpg" width="500" height="100"></td>
  </tr>
  <tr>
    <td height="100"><img src="form_jump03.jpg" width="500" height="100"></td>
  </tr>
  <tr>
    <td height="100"><img src="form_jump04.jpg" width="500" height="100"></td>
  </tr>
  <tr>
    <td height="100" background="form_jump05.jpg"><form name="form1">
      <select name="menu1" onChange="MM_jumpMenu('parent',this,0)">
        <option value="http://www.macromedia.com" selected>macromedia</option>
        <option value="http://www.yahoo.com">yahoo</option>
      </select>
    </form>
    </td>
  </tr>
</table>
</body>
</html>
```

You can easily add a jump menu via HTML by inserting <option> tags for each selection within a <select> tag, as shown below. To remove a jump menu, simply delete the corresponding code.

```
<select name="menu1" onChange="MM_jumpMenu('parent',this,0)">
        <option value="http://www.macromedia.com" selected>macromedia</option>
        <option value="http://www.yahoo.com">yahoo</option>
        <option value="http://www.as.wiley.com">wiley</option>
        <option value="http://www.hp.com">hp</option>
</select>
```

A Web site featuring a jump menu

Another example of a jump menu

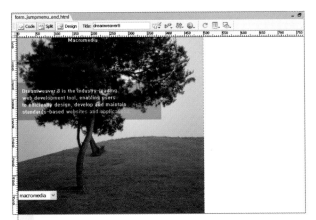

6 You can see that the jump menu has been inserted; "macromedia" is displayed because it was inserted first.

7 Save the document and press F12 to preview it. Check the document in a Web browser.

2 Creating a Member Registration Page

A member registration page is an essential page on many Web sites. It may consist of only one page, but often there are several member registration pages as well as a preview page to be completed before member information is sent to the server. In this example, we will create some typical member registration pages and learn how to insert and configure form elements.

Start File
\Sample\06_file\form_register.htm

Final File
\Sample\06_file\form_register_end.htm

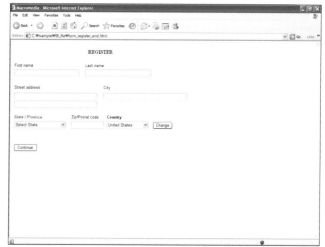

Final page

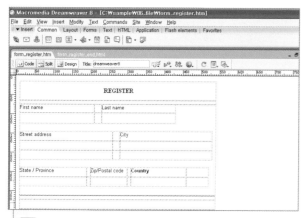

1 Open the file \Sample\ 06_file\form_register.htm. We will insert form elements into the basic table and define their properties.

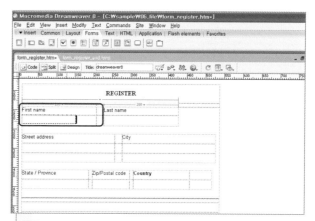

2 Move the mouse cursor into the cell immediately below First name. Select Forms > Text Field from the Insert bar and insert a text field into the cell.

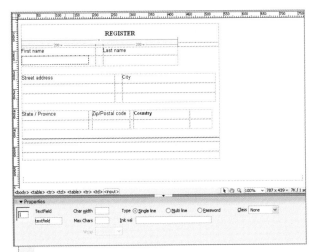

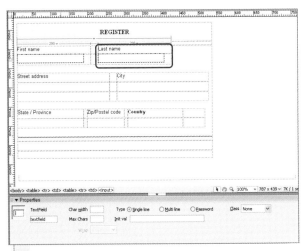

3 Click the inserted text field. In the Properties inspector at the bottom of the Dreamweaver window, set 30 for Char width (the width of the text field expressed in number of characters) and 64 for Max Chars (the maximum number of characters that can be inserted into the text field).

4 Select the inserted text field and press Ctrl-C to copy it. Paste it into the cell immediately below Last name. Do not change the properties of the new text field.

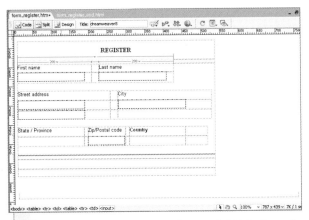

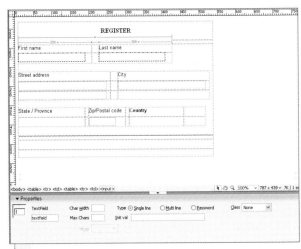

5 In the same manner, paste the text field into the cells below Street address, City, and Zip/Postal code.

6 Change the properties of the fields inserted under Street address, City, and Zip/Postal code using the values below.

note >>>

Text Field Properties for Step 6
Street address: Char width: 40, Max Char: 100
City: Char width: 40, Max Char: 100
Zip/Postal code: Char width: 12, Max Char: 12

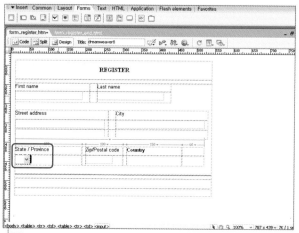

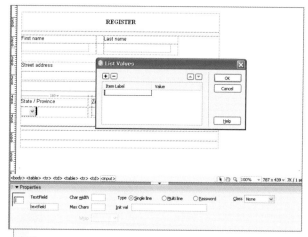

7 To insert a list or menu below State/Province and Country, select the cell below State/Province and select Forms > List/Menu from the Insert bar.

8 Select the list/menu and then click the List Values button in the Properties inspector to open the List Values dialog box.

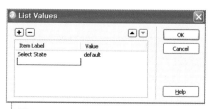

9 In the List Values dialog box, enter "Select State" for Item Label and "default" for Value. Click the ⊞ button to enter values for the other list items, as shown below. Then click the OK button.

Item Label	Value
Select State	Default
Alabama	AL
Alaska	AK
Arizona	AZ

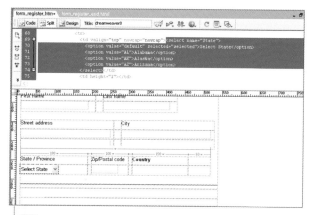

10 Select Split so that you can check the inserted code.

```
<select name="select">
          <option    value="default"
selected="selected">Select State</option>
   <option value="AL">Alabama</option>
   <option value="AK">Alaska</option>
   <option value="AZ">Arizona</option>
</select>
```

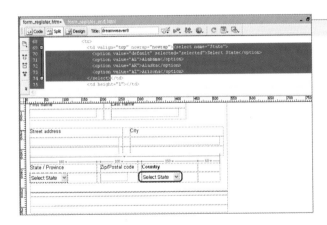

11 If you have a little knowledge of HTML code, you can produce Web registration pages more quickly. First, select the list/menu under State/Province and press Ctrl-C to copy it. Then paste it into the cell below Country by pressing Ctrl-V.

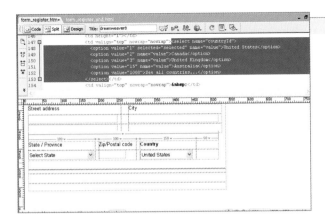

12 Select the list/menu below Country and change the code in Code view as shown below.

[Before change]

```
<select name="select2">
            <option     value="default"
selected="selected">Select State</option>
    <option value="AL">Alabama</option>
    <option value="AK">Alaska</option>
    <option value="AZ">Arizona</option>
</select>
```

[After change]

```
<select name="countryId">
    <option value="1" selected="selected" name="value">United States</option>
    <option value="2" name="value">Canada</option>
    <option value="3" name="value">United Kingdom</option>
    <option value="15" name="value">Australia</option>
    <option value="1000">See all countries...</option>
</select>
```

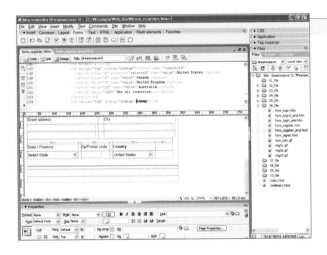

13 Insert a button in the cell to the right of the list/menu. Move the mouse cursor into the cell and select Forms > Button from the Insert bar.

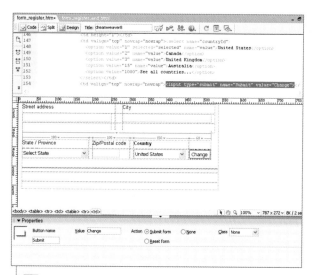

14 Select the inserted button and enter "Change" for Value in the Properties inspector.

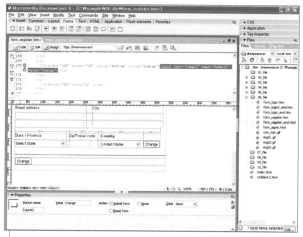

15 Select the button and press Ctrl-C to copy it. Then paste it into the cell below it by pressing Ctrl-V.

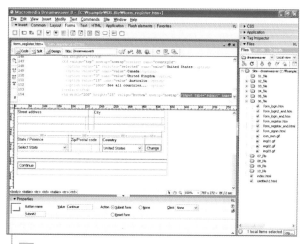

16 Change Value to "Continue" in the Properties inspector.

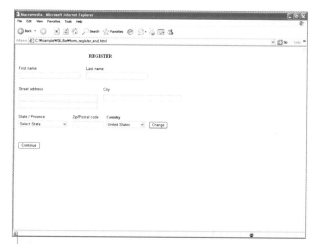

17 Save the edited document and press the F12 key to preview it.

Creating a Login Page

It is simpler to create a login page than the member registration page described in the previous exercise. However, you need to display various responses depending on the user's behavior, which makes this more than just a page for entering an ID and password. For example, if users enter the wrong ID or password, they should be notified. In this exercise, we will create both a login page and the page that appears when the wrong ID or password is entered.

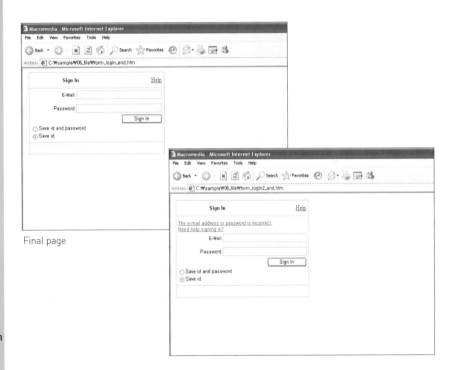

Final page

Start File
  \Sample\06_file\form_login.htm

Final Files
  \Sample\06_file\form_login_end.htm
  \Sample\06_file\form_login2_end.htm

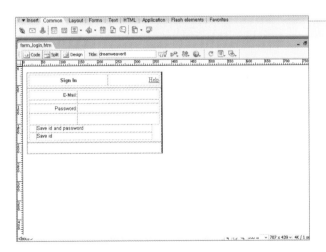

1 Open the file \Sample\06_file\form_login.htm.

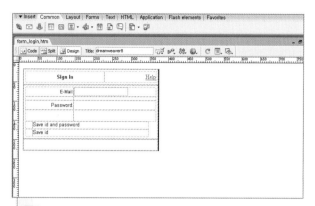

2　As shown, move the mouse cursor into the cell beside E-mail and select Forms > Text Field from the Insert bar.

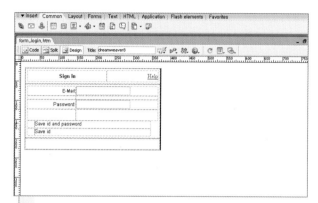

3　When the text field has been inserted, select it and then copy it by pressing Ctrl-C. Paste it into the cell beside Password by pressing Ctrl-V.

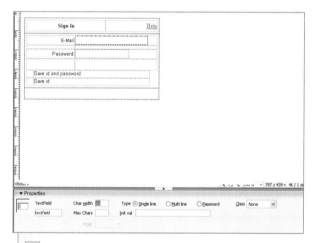

4　After the two text fields are inserted, change the properties of each text field. First, select the text field inserted for E-mail and enter 30 for Char width in the Properties inspector.

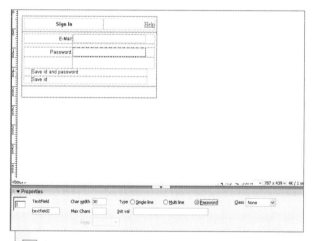

5　Select the text field inserted for Password and enter 30 for Char width and "Password" for Type in the Properties inspector.

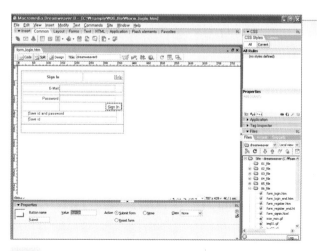

6　Move the mouse cursor into the cell below Password and select Forms > Button from the Insert bar. Select the inserted button and enter "Sign In" for Value.

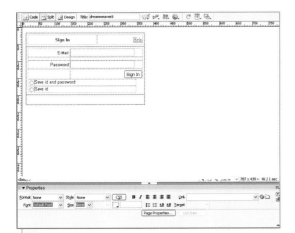

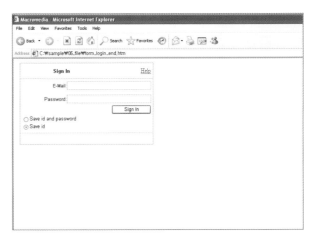

7 Select Forms > Radio Button from the Insert bar to insert a radio button in each empty cell below and to the left of the Sign In button to complete the login page. Then save the edited document and press the F12 key to preview it.

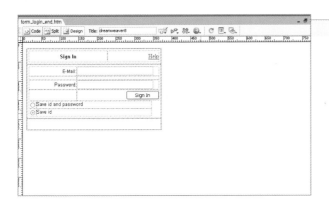

8 The page created above is a login page. Now we will create a page that will be displayed when the wrong information is entered. Open the file form_login_end.htm.

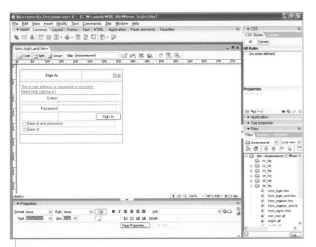

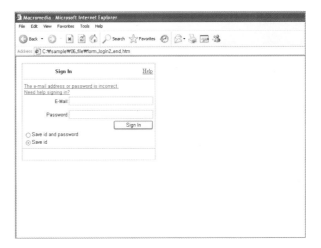

9 Create a table with three rows above the e-mail input form and enter the text shown at right. Then save it under a new name. Once you've created these two pages, a Web programmer can write the program that's required to determine which version of the site users see (based on their entries).

note >>>

Text for Step 8

The e-mail address or password is incorrect. Please retype the e-mail address and password, or sign up if you haven't already done so. Need help signing in?

Chapter 7

Laying Out Pages with CSSs

HTML is simpler and easier to learn and use than server script languages. However, it also has limitations when used by itself. For example, it is impossible to make changes to a background image, change a form style, or alter the shape of a mouse pointer by using HTML. To overcome such limitations, cascading style sheets were introduced with the HTML 3.2 standard. In this chapter, we will learn how to lay out Web pages effectively using CSSs.

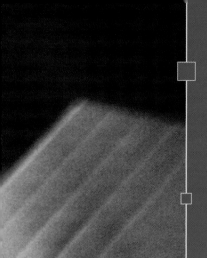

Working with CSSs

T here are only so many things you can do with HTML. In this section we'll discuss how you can use CSSs to supplement your work in HTML to create more dynamic Web sites.

What are CSSs?

CSSs enable you to control detailed properties that cannot be controlled with HTML tags, such as line height, repetition count for background images, roll-over text in menus, and dotted lines in tables. You can think of them as "smart" bits of code that dynamically regulate elements of your pages. They offer numerous advantages when designing sites:

- You can implement various styles that would not be possible with HTML tags alone.
- You can save styles as CSS format files, and apply them to many different documents.
- You can apply one style sheet to an entire Web site to give it a sense of unity.
- You can update the source code of a style sheet, and apply it to all documents at once to save update time.

Style sheets can be inserted between the <HEAD> and </HEAD> tags in an HTML document in the following manner:

```
<style type=""text/css">
<!--
body {
margin-left: 0px;
margin-top: 0px;
margin-right: 0px;
margin-bottom: 0px;
}
-->
</style>
```

For external style sheets, just insert the link source for a style sheet between the <HEAD> and </HEAD> tags, without using the "<style type=""text/css">" and "</style>" tags.

```
<link href="css.css" rel="stylesheet" type="text/css"
```

150

Types of Style Sheets

Style sheets can be classified into three different types, depending on their scope and target. Each of the three types is described below.

Custom Style Sheets

Web designers can define the name of a style sheet, then use it in a document by inserting the HTML class="style sheet name" into the tag of the object to which the style should be applied (see the sample code to the right). Custom style sheets are widely used because you can directly control their application. To use this feature in Dreamweaver, select "Class" under Selector Type from the New CSS Rule dialog box.

```
.dot {
border: 1px dotted #FFCCFF;
}

<span class="red" <hr> </span>
```

HTML Redefining Style Sheets

These style sheets change or add to the properties of HTML tags. For example, when you use a style sheet to redefine the <li> tag for listing items, the change is automatically applied to all lists inserted in a document. To use this feature in Dreamweaver, insert the style as shown in HTML tag format, and select "Tag" under Selector Type from the New CSS Rule dialog box.

```
li {
font-family: "Arial";
font-size; 9pt;
line-height: 120%;
list-style-image; url(images/li.gif);
}
```

Linked Style Sheets

Linked Style Sheets control the properties of hyperlinks. You can change or add to the properties of a hyperlink according to its state, for example link, visited, active, and hover. To use this feature in Dreamweaver, insert the style in the format "a:state" as shown, and select "Advanced" under Selector Type from the New CSS Rule dialog box.

```
a:link {
text-decoration: none;
}
a:visited {
text-decoration: none;
}
a:hover {
text-decoration: none;
color; #FFFFFF;
background-color: #000000;
}
a:active {
text-decoration: none;
color: #000000;
}
```

The Default CSS Setting in Dreamweaver

When you first install and start Dreamweaver, CSSs are applied automatically by default. This is very convenient and saves a lot of effort. However, it presents an unfamiliar work environment because working with CSSs is different than working in HTML. Consequently, rather than using CSSs automatically created by Dreamweaver, it is better to directly create and control CSSs at first so that you can attain some familiarity with how they work. We will now change Dreamweaver's default setting so that you can create and use CSSs manually.

❶ Start Dreamweaver and press Ctrl-U. The Preferences dialog box appears.

❷ In the General category of the Preferences dialog box, deselect Use CSS instead of HTML tags. (With this option selected, CSSs would be automatically applied.)

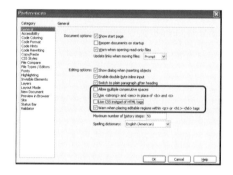

❸ Now you can manipulate the properties of text, for instance, manually. (This was the default setting in the previous version of Dreamweaver.)

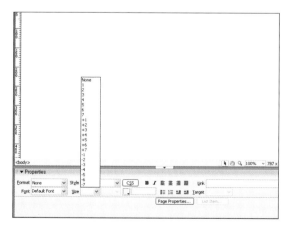

152

Inserting CSSs

There are two methods for inserting CSSs in Dreamweaver: directly inserting a CSS in Code view or using the CSS Styles panel. To insert a CSS in Code view, you must understand the structure of the CSS and type the source code in directly. Needless to say, this is not a job for beginners! On the other hand, the CSS Styles panel allows you to easily control a CSS if you know its basic features. Moreover, you can conveniently manage any style sheets you've created from the CSS Styles panel.

The CSS Styles Panel

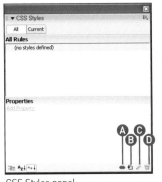

CSS Styles panel

Adding new CSSs in the CSS Styles panel

Ⓐ Attach Style Sheet: Connects a style sheet in file format (*.css) to the Web page on which you are currently working.

Ⓑ New CSS Rule: Creates a new style sheet.

Ⓒ Edit Style Sheet: Enables you to edit a selected style sheet.

Ⓓ Delete CSS Rule: Deletes a selected style sheet.

Creating CSSs

By creating your own style sheets, you can fully customize Dreamweaver's CSS features. In this way, you can design your page templates down to the finest detail. For example, you can determine the style of boxes, add rollover effects to text, and design your own font palettes.

The New CSS Rule Dialog Box

When you click the New CSS Rule button in the CSS Styles panel, the New CSS Rule dialog box appears.

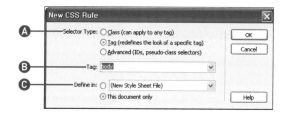

A Selector Type: Choose one of the following three methods for applying the CSS:

- Class: This is used to create a Custom Style Sheet.

- Tag: This is used to create an HTML Redefining Style Sheet.

- Advanced: CSSs are applied to linked content in the page by default, but you can also apply CSSs using Class by specifying a separate name.

B Tag: Different options appear depending on the selector type.

C Define in: Choose between the following methods of saving the CSS:

New Style Sheet File: A CSS file (*.css) is created and saved. Choose this option when the same CSS is to be applied to different pages or documents.

This Document Only: Use this method if the CSS is to be inserted in and applied to only the current HTML document.

Using CSSs to Edit Web Sites Globally

When you create multiple Web pages, the CSSs inserted into subpages are usually almost identical to one another. You can apply one CSS to all pages, or, if you create a CSS file, you can connect it and insert it into any or all pages and manage each separately. In this way, CSS files are also convenient for editing existing Web sites. If you were not using a CSS file and needed to apply style changes throughout a site, you would have to edit each page individually. With a CSS file, you just need to change its properties once. This is not such an important feature if you are working with a small number of pages, but for a Web site with many pages, it is essential to use CSS files.

1

Creating and Applying a CSS

The first step toward mastering CSSs is learning how to make and use them. In this exercise we'll walk you through the process.

Start File
> \Sample\07_file\css_01.htm

Final File
> \Sample\07_file\css_01_end.htm

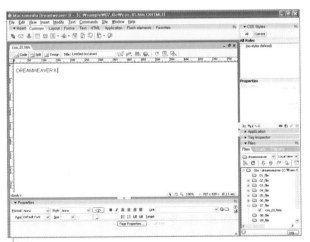 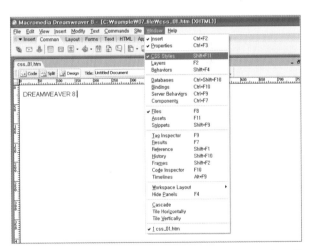

1 Open the file \Sample\07_file\css_01.htm. The CSS Styles panel appears to the right of the Dreamweaver window. If the CSS Styles panel does not appear, select Window > CSS Styles from the Menu bar.

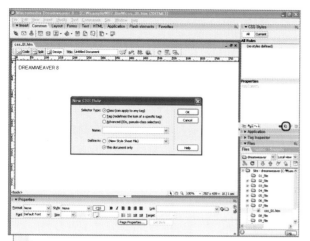

note >>>

Settings for Step 3

Selector Type: Class

Name: .text01 (be sure to enter "." in front of the name)

Define in: New Style Sheet File

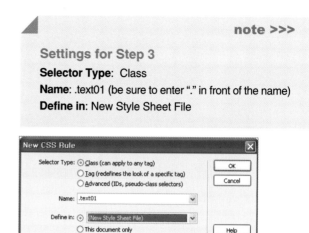

2 Click the New CSS Rule button in the CSS Styles panel. The New CSS Rule dialog box appears.

3 Enter the values shown below in the New CSS Rule dialog box and click the OK button.

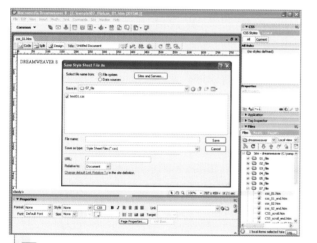

4 As shown in the figure, when the Save Style Sheet File As dialog box appears, select the CSS format and a filename. Here we will save it as "text01.css."

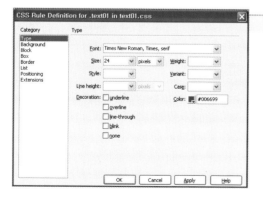

5 Now a dialog box appears that allows you to select formatting, as shown in the figure. You can enter the CSS style you want. Enter the values given below in the Type category and click the OK button.

note >>>

Settings for Step 5

Font: Times New Roman, Times, serif

Size: 24 pixels

Color: #006699

6 Click the New CSS Rule button in the CSS Styles panel. The New CSS Rule dialog box appears.

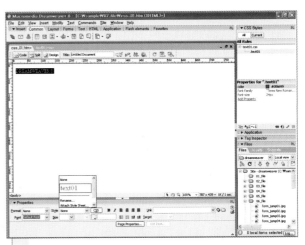

7 To apply the style sheet, first select the text. Then select text01 from Style in the Properties inspector.

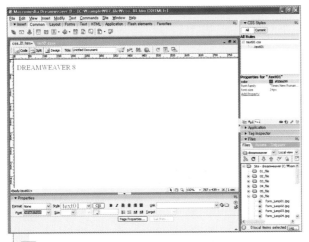

8 You can see in this figure that the style has been applied to the selection.

9 Save the file and press F12 to preview it.

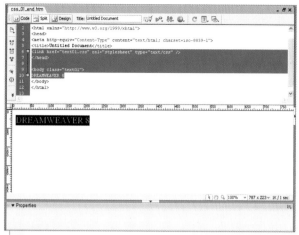

10 Check the source code for the inserted CSS in Dreamweaver. Click the Split button to see Code view and Design view at the same time.

11 Select File > Open from the Menu bar to open the file text01.css. Then check the content of the CSS.

```
<html  xmlns="http://www.w3.org/1999 /xhtml">
<head>
<meta http equiv="Content Type" content
="text/html; charset=iso 8859 1">
<title>Untitled Document</title>
<link href="text01.css" rel="stylesheet"
type="text/css" />
</head>
<body class="text01">
DREAMWEAVER 8
</body>
</html>
```

```
.text01 {
      font   family: "Times New Roman",
Times, serif;
      font  size: 24px;
      color: #006699;
}
```

Applying a CSS to the Current Page Only

Sometimes, you may want to apply a CSS to a single page on a Web site, as opposed to every page on the site. In the following steps, we will apply a CSS in the <head> tag to achieve this.

Start File
\Sample\Chapter07\css_02.htm

Final File
\Sample\Chapter07\css_02_end.htm

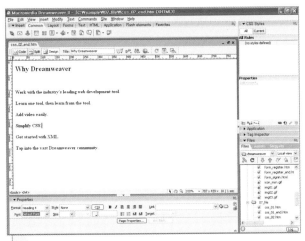

1 Start Dreamweaver and open the file \Sample\ 07_file\css_02.htm.

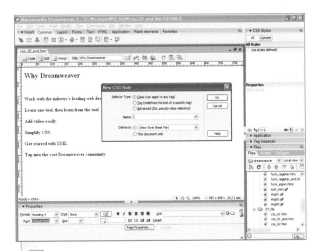

2 Click the New CSS Rule button from the CSS Styles panel. The New CSS Rule dialog box appears.

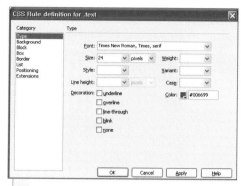

3 Select these options in the New CSS Rule dialog box and click the OK button.

4 When the formatting dialog box appears, select Type for Category. Enter the values given below in Type and click the OK button.

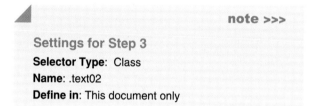

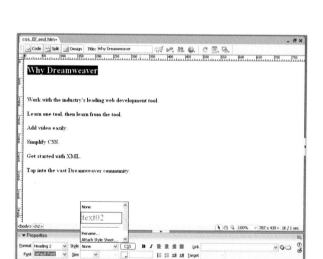

5 Now insert the created style sheet. First, select the text to which you want to apply the CSS. Then select text02 from Style in the Properties inspector.

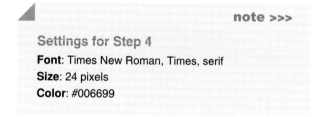

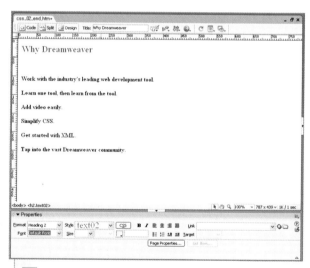

6 You can see that the CSS has been applied.

7 Check the source code of the applied CSS in Code view. There are more lines of code than was the case when a separate CSS file was used.

```
<html xmlns="http://www.w3.org/1999/xhtml">
<head>
<meta http equiv="Content Type" content="text/html; charset=iso 8859 1">
<title>Why Dreamweaver</title>
<style type="text/css">
<!
.text02 {
        font family: "Times New Roman", Times, serif;
        font size: 24px;
        color: #006699;
}
    >
</style>
</head>


<body>
<h2 class="text02">Why Dreamweaver</h2>
<h4> </h4>
<h4>Work with the industry's leading web development tool.</h4>
<h4>Learn one tool, then learn from the tool.</h4>
<h4>Add video easily.</h4>
<h4>Simplify CSS.</h4>
<h4>Get started with XML.</h4>
<h4>Tap into the vast Dreamweaver community.</h4>
</body>
</html>
```

3

Looking at the CSSs of Famous Sites

Most Web sites use CSSs to present and manage text and other content. In addition, Web sites that have many pages usually manage styles with CSS files. In this exercise, we will check the CSSs of famous Web sites because much can be learned from the way they are organized. Note that while it is possible to view the CSSs of most sites, some sites won't let you see their source code.

Web Site
http://www.adobe.com/

Sample page

1 Start your Web browser and go to http://www.adobe.com/.

2 To find the path of the site's CSS files, we will view the HTML source code. Select View > Source from the Menu bar of your Web browser.

Absolute Paths and Relative Paths

Web-based content must be uploaded to a server connected to the Internet. To show the uploaded content in a Web browser, you must specify the path of each element in the site. The paths of content can be classified as absolute paths or relative paths.

- Absolute path: The whole path of the file, starting from the server, is specified (e.g., http://www.yahoo.com/image/main.jpg).

- Relative path: The path of the file is specified from the current folder (e.g., image/main.jpg).

3 The HTML source code of the selected page opens in Notepad.

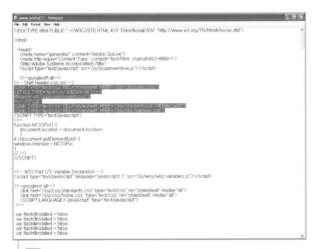

4 Typically the HTML source for inserting a CSS file is in the <head> tag. Check the CSS file path in the <head> tag in Notepad. You can see that the CSS file paths are not absolute paths but relative paths. See the sample code below for a closer look.

5 When you start Dreamweaver and enter the absolute path of the CSS file in the Web browser, the CSS file is opened in Dreamweaver. First, combine the current domain name with the relative path /ssi/css/basic.css and enter it in your Web browser. Now hit Enter.

```
<LINK TYPE="text/css" REL="stylesheet" HREF="/ssi/css/basic.css">
<STYLE TYPE="text/css" MEDIA="all"><!--@import url("/ssi/css/modern.css");--></STYLE>
<LINK TYPE="text/css" REL="stylesheet" HREF="/ssi/css/print.css" MEDIA="print">
<LINK TYPE="text/css" REL="stylesheet" HREF="/ssi/css/mainnav.css">
```

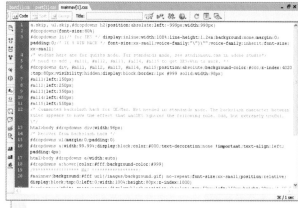

6 There is no change in the Web browser. However, the basic.css file opens in Dreamweaver.

7 Open other CSS files in this same way by using the absolute paths of the files. Review the CSS for clues about how the site is constructed. The programmers and designers behind commercial Web sites are almost always highly skilled pros. Since they build pages for a living, they often develop tricks, workarounds, or creative solutions to complex problems, and much can be learned by reviewing their work. If you find yourself stumped or looking for creative new ways to build a site, dig around online and find inspiring sites that are already live. You never know what you might pick up by peeking into their code.

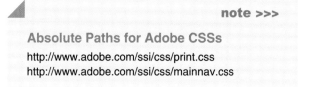

note >>>

Absolute Paths for Adobe CSSs

http://www.adobe.com/ssi/css/print.css
http://www.adobe.com/ssi/css/mainnav.css

tip >>

Viewing HTML Source Code

There are several methods for checking the HTML source code of Web pages shown in a Web browser. Although some Web sites prohibit general users from viewing their HTML source code, generally you can check the HTML source of most Web sites. There are three methods of viewing the HTML source code.

❶ Select View > Source from the Menu bar of your Web browser. The HTML source code opens in Notepad.

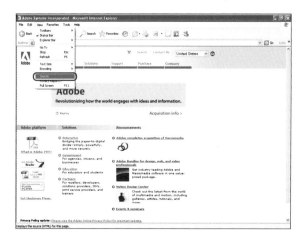

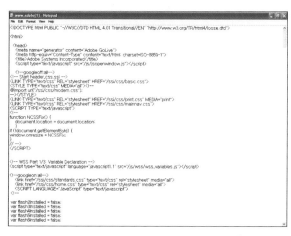

continue ▶ ▶ ▶

❷ Right-click your mouse in the Web browser and click View
Source from the pop-up menu to open the HTML source
code in Notepad.

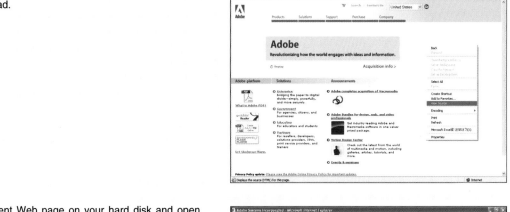

❸ Save the current Web page on your hard disk and open
the HTML document. Select File > Save from the Menu
bar of the Web browser to save the current page to your
hard disk. Then open the saved document in
Dreamweaver or Notepad. When you use this method,
JavaScript and CSS files are downloaded, as well.

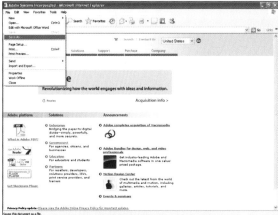

4 Creating Rollover Effects in Tables

You can use CSSs as a simple method for applying various effects to text and tables. For example, you can set the thickness and color of table borders individually, or have the background color of a table change in response to a mouse event. In this example, we will create a rollover effect in a table.

Start File
\Sample\07_file\css_table.htm

Final File
\Sample\07_file\css_table_end.htm

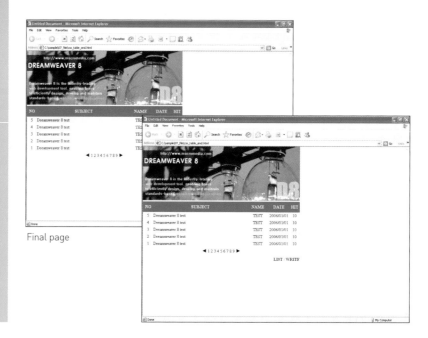

Final page

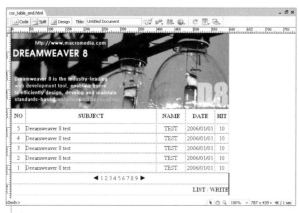

1 Open the file \Sample\ 07_file\css_table.htm.

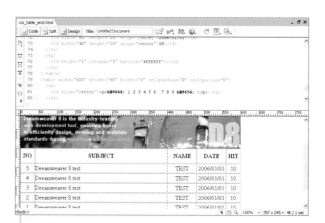

2 Click the Split button to see Code view and Design view at the same time.

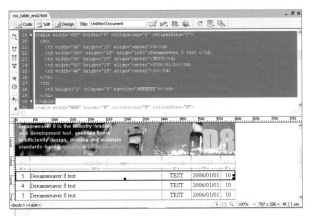

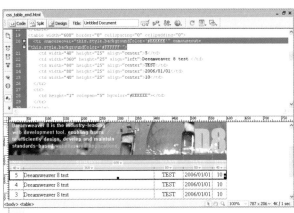

3 Select the #5 table row in Design view, as shown in the figure. The source code of the table is selected in Code view as well.

4 Change the content of the first <tr> of the selected table in Code view as shown below.

```
<tr  onmouseover="this.style.backgroundColor=
'#EEEEEE'"  onmouseout="this.style.background
Color='#FFFFFF'">
```

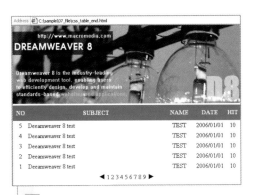

5 Save the edited document and press the F12 key to preview it. Notice that when you move your mouse pointer over the row, its background color changes.

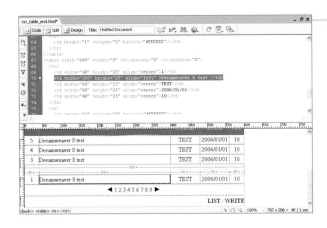

6 In the procedure just described, we used the <tr> tag, and the event affected the whole <tr>, or table row. Now we can insert the same source code within the <td> tag to create a mouse event effect in just one cell. In row #1, select the cell that contains "Dreamweaver 8 test."

167

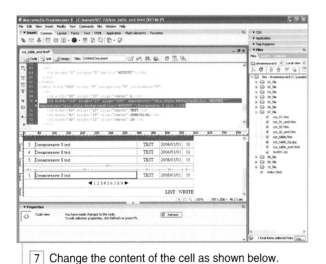

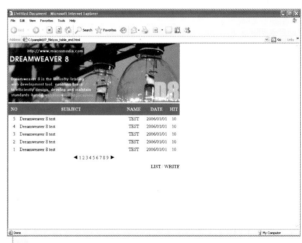

7 Change the content of the cell as shown below.

8 Save the edited document and press the F12 key to preview it. When you move your mouse pointer to the cell, the background color of only that cell changes.

```
<td width="360" height="25" align="left"
onmouseover="this.style.backgroundColor='#EEE
EEE'" onmouseout="this.style.backgroundColor=
'#FFFFFF'">
```

tip >>

Changing Table Background Colors and Working with Mouse Events

A background color change may be applied independently by using <table>, <tr>, or <td>. That is, you can choose to change the background color of the whole table, of the whole table row, or, individually, each cell.

For this purpose, we can use the following two mouse events:

- onmouseover: When the mouse pointer is over the selected object.
- onmouseout: When the mouse pointer moves away from the selected object.

Additional mouse events may or may not be available to users, depending on their Web browsers. A variety of events can be used in recent versions of Web browsers while only limited events can be used in older versions. You can review those events in Dreamweaver from the Behavior pull-down menu.

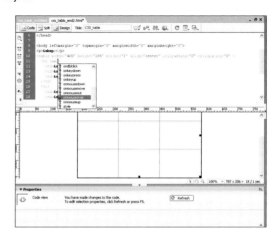

When you enter a tag in Code view, the options for the tag are provided by Dreamweaver. For example, when you enter "<table"and press the Space key, a drop-down menu with the options for the table tag appears below the mouse cursor. When you select an option, it is automatically inserted into the code.

168

5

Changing the Shape and Color of Scroll Bars

Another important feature of CSSs is that they allow you to alter the shape and color of scroll bars. This a great way to give your pages a unique look. In this exercise, we will change the shape and color of scroll bars using CSSs.

Start File
\Sample\07_file\CSS_scroll.htm

Final File
\Sample\07_file\CSS_scroll_end.htm

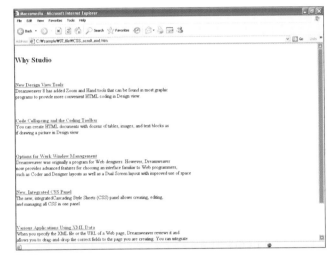

Final page

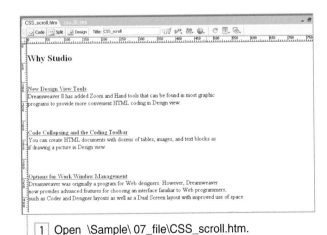

1 Open \Sample\ 07_file\CSS_scroll.htm.

2 When the file opens, click the Split button to see Code view and Design view at the same time.

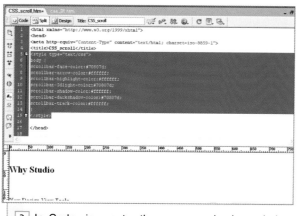

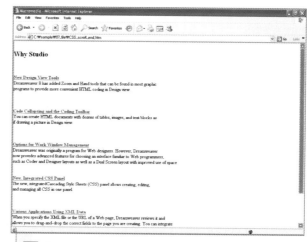

3 In Code view, enter the source code shown below between the tags <head> and </head>.

4 Select File > Save from the Menu bar to save the edited document. Press the F12 key to preview it. You can see the new scroll bar color in this figure.

```
<style type="text/css">
body {
scrollbar   face   color:#70807d;
scrollbar   arrow   color:#ffffff;
scrollbar   highlight   color:#ffffff;
scrollbar   3dlight   color:#70807d;
scrollbar   shadow   color:#ffffff;
scrollbar   darkshadow   color:#70807d;
scrollbar   track   color:#ffffff;
}
</style>
```

tip >>

Scroll Bar Properties

The CSS control properties for scroll bars are described below.

Scrollbar face color:	Determines the inner color of buttons and scroll bar
Scrollbar arrow color:	Determines the arrow color of buttons
Scrollbar highlight color:	Determines the middle color of buttons
Scrollbar 3dlight color:	Determines the outer color of buttons
Scrollbar shadow color:	Determines the shadow color of buttons
Scrollbar darkshadow color:	Determines the inner color of buttons and scroll bar
Scrollbar track color:	Determines the background color of the area in which the scroll bar moves

The "Make a Document XHTML-compliant" Setting

If the scroll bar of the Web browser does not show a change, delete the content of "Make a document XHTML-compliant" from the HTML source. In Dreamweaver, "Make a document XHTML-compliant" is selected by default, and it can cause problems.

```
<!DOCTYPE html PUBLIC "  //W3C//DTD XHTML 1.0 Strict//EN" "http://www.w3.org/TR/xhtml1/DTD
/xhtml1  strict.dtd">
<html xmlns="http://www.w3.org/1999/xhtml">
<head>
<meta http equiv="Content  Type" content="text/html; charset=euc  kr" />
<title>Untitled Document</title>
</head>
<body>
</body>
</html>
```

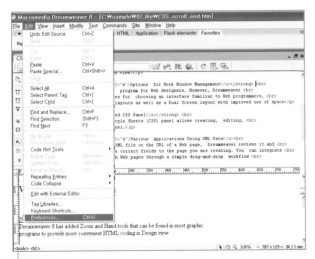

5 To deselect the Make a document XHTML-compliant option, select Edit > Preferences from the Menu bar in Dreamweaver.

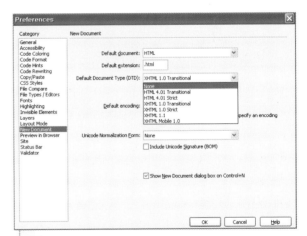

6 In the Preferences dialog box, select None as the Default Document Type in the New Document category. Then click the OK button.

171

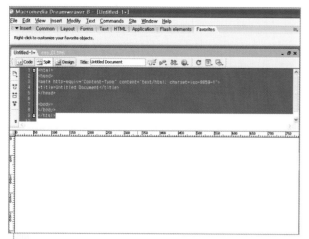

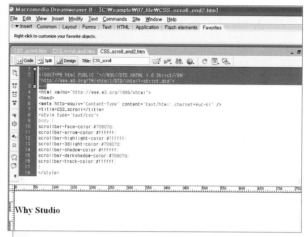

7 Select File > New from the Menu bar to create a new document. You can see in the figure that the Make a document XHTML-compliant setting code is not present. See the code below for reference.

```
<html>
<head>
<meta    http    equiv="Content    Type"
content="text/html; charset=iso  8859  1">
<title>Untitled Document</title>
</head>
<body>
</body>
</html>
```

8 You can often use this method to solve problems associated with CSSs. Alternatively, you can simply alter the HTML of problematic code so that it is read as a comment by the Web browser (comments are purely for reference and are ignored by the browser). The benefit of this technique is that it's very fast and you don't have to alter any of Dreamweaver's default settings. See the sample code below for a demo.

```
<!
<!DOCTYPE html PUBLIC "  //W3C//DTD XHTML 1.0
Strict//EN" "http://www.w3.org/TR/xhtml1/DTD/
xhtml1  strict.dtd">
-->
```

172

6

Completing the Member Registration Page

In general, CSSs are indispensable when producing pages that contain text elements. With CSSs, you can control not only fixed text but also text that changes in response to mouse events. In this exercise, we will insert CSSs into a basic membership registration page.

Start File
\Sample\07_file\from_register_end2.htm

Final File
\Sample\07_file\from_register_end.htm

Final page

1 Open the file \Sample\ 07_file\form_register_end2.htm.

2 To create a new CSS, open the CSS panel and click the New CSS Rule icon.

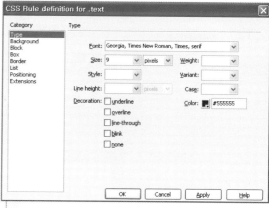

3 When the New CSS Rule dialog box appears, enter the values shown below and click the OK button.

4 When the formatting dialog box appears, enter the values shown below and click the OK button.

note >>>

Settings for Step 3
Selector Type: Class
Name: .text
Define in: This document only

note >>>

Settings for Step 4
Font: Georgia, Times New Roman, Times, serif
Size: 9 pixels
Color: #555555

tip >>

Choosing Text Colors

It is important to choose text colors that will appeal to the users of the Web site. It is recommended that you not use primary colors for text when producing general sites. Using primary colors improves legibility but may also cause eye fatigue. If Web sites cause such fatigue, visitors won't stay for long, so use primary colors only in places that really require them. The most important task is to find out who the actual visitors are and use the right colors for them.

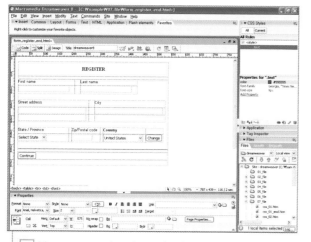

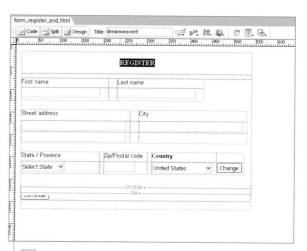

5 You can see that the style sheet has been inserted in the CSS panel, as shown in the figure.

6 Select REGISTER and select Style > Text in the Properties inspector.

174

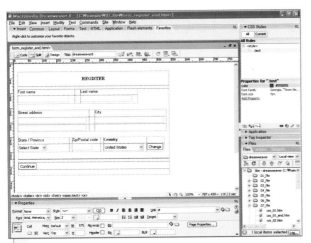

7 You can see that the style has been applied to the selection. Apply the CSS to other text selections, or create additional CSSs to mix things up.

Advanced CSS Techniques

One of the most frequently used applications of CSSs is to format text links. CSSs even allow you to apply effects to text links based on mouse events.

Formatting Text Links

CSSs used to format links may be applied to whole pages or parts of pages. Dreamweaver supports both applications, but the methods for each are a little different.

01 First, to apply a CSS to all the links on a page, open the New CSS Rule dialog box, select Advanced as the Selector Type, and then a:link as the Selector.

02 This CSS is then applied to all the links on the page. It is displayed in the CSS Styles panel but not in the Properties inspector.

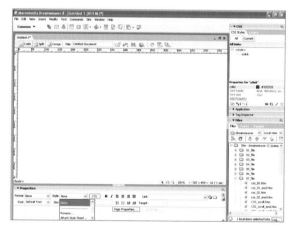

03 To apply a CSS to individual links, select Advanced and then change Selector from a:link to a.han:link.

04 The CSS "han" is created in the Properties inspector, and you can apply it to any links you choose.

Adding Rollover Effects to Links

You can go a step further and use CSSs to create rollover effects for text links. In this exercise, we'll show you how, and introduce some of the quirks that arise when you're working with CSSs and HTML tags.

01 Start Dreamweaver and enter the text shown below in Design view.

02 You can add links to all text elements without setting a specific address. Here we specified "#" in the address window. Click the Split button to see Code view and Design view at the same time.

note >>>

Text for Step 01
1. Dreamweaver 8
2. Flash 8
3. Fireworks 8

03 Select Advanced in the New CSS Rule dialog box. Then select a:hover (for Selector) and This document only (for Define in), and click the OK button.

04 Selector a:hover refers to the CSS when a mouse hovers over the text. Set the values given below and click the OK button.

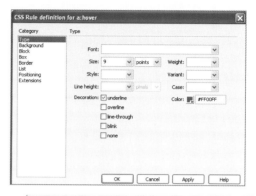

note >>>

Settings for Step 04
Font size: 9pt
Color: #FF00FF
Text decoration: underline

05 Open the New CSS Rule dialog box again and select Advanced. Then select a:link (for Selector) and This document only (for Define in), and click the OK button.

06 Select the rule definitions shown below. Then click the OK button.

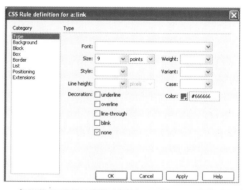

note >>>

Settings for Step 06
Size: 9 points
Color: #666666
Decoration: none

07 Lastly, open the New CSS Rule dialog box. Select a:visited (for Selector) and make other settings identical to those for a:link.

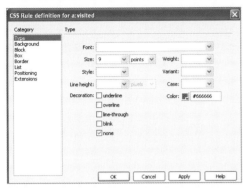

> note >>>
>
> ### Settings for Step 07
> **Size**: 9 points
> **Color**: #666666
> **Decoration**: none

09 You will see that there is a problem with a:hover; there is no change when you move the mouse over the text. This problem can be solved by changing the order of a:hover, a:link, and a:visited in Code view, as shown below.

08 Select File > Save from the Menu bar to save the edited document and press the F12 key to preview it.

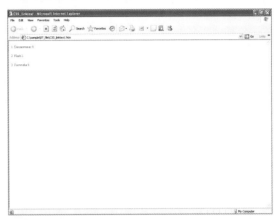

Before change

```
a:hover {
        font  size: 9pt;
        color: #FF00FF;
        text  decoration: underline;
}
a:link {
        font  size: 9pt;
        color: #666666;
        text  decoration: none;
}
a:visited {
        font  size: 9pt;
        color: #666666;
        text  decoration: none;
}
```

After change

```
a:visited {
        font  size: 9pt;
        color: #666666;
        text  decoration: none;
}
a:hover {
        font  size: 9pt;
        color: #FF00FF;
        text  decoration: underline;
}
a:link {
        font  size: 9pt;
        color: #666666;
        text  decoration: none;
}
```

10 In Design view, select "2. Flash 8" with your mouse and specify green (#00FF00) for Color in the Properties inspector. One caution: You should check whether the HTML tags are correct in Code view. If the code reads "<font color="#00FF00"><a href="#">2. Flash 8</a></font>" it will not be applied in Design view. The text color will change only when the code reads "<a href="#"><font color="#00FF00">2. Flash 8</font></a>".

11 Now select "3. Fireworks 8" with your mouse and specify Color as #FF6600 in the Properties inspector. As in the previous step, check whether the HTML tags are correctly set as "<a href="#"><font color="#FF6600">3. Fireworks 8</font></a>". If not, you should directly change the code in Code view.

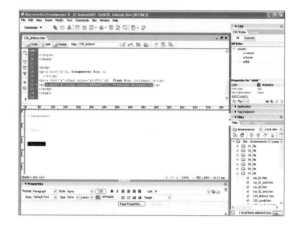

12 Press F12 to preview the document. As shown in the figure, when you move your mouse over "1. Dreamweaver 8" its text color changes, and the text is underlined due to the HTML code, "text decoration: underline;".

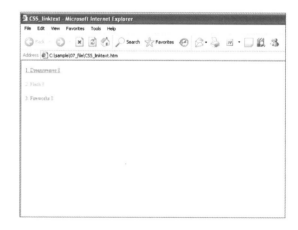

13 Note that the color specified in the a:link CSS has not been applied to the Flash and Dreamweaver links. This is because the HTML colors we applied to these links (in their <font> tags> are interpreted by the Web browser before the CSS instructions. Essentially, the HTML cancels out the CSS color formatting. Since there is no HTML tag competing with the underline aspect of the a:link formatting, this part of the CSS still works for these links.

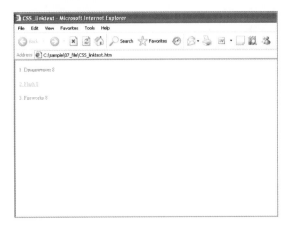

14 If you change "<a href="#"><font color="#FF6600">3. Fire</font>works 8</a>" to "<a href="#"><font color="#FF6600">3. Fireworks 8</font></a>", the underline color will change along with the text color, as shown here. This happens because you've removed "works 8" from the <font> tag, so the CSS formatting is allowed to affect this part of the link.

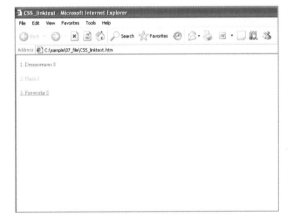

Chapter | 8

Using Behaviors to Create Dynamic Web Sites

Web sites are changing from static places to dynamic ones that respond to users' behavior. Dreamweaver provides behavior options that enable you to create dynamic Web sites in which mouse clicks alone can result in dynamic output. This chapter describes what behaviors are and how to use them.

The Basic Properties of Behaviors

For many Web designers, JavaScript creates a formidable barrier between the creation of an attractive user interface and a fully functional, interactive Web paradise. Dreamweaver offers a simple solution: behaviors. In this section, we'll cover the basics, then move on to some exercises so you can see behaviors in action.

Behavior Basics

Interactive Web sites depend heavily on JavaScript; this is the most universal programming language used on the Web. Unfortunately, JavaScript isn't exactly easy to learn. Dreamweaver aids would-be Web designers by allowing them to use JavaScript without having to write it themselves. This is where behaviors come in.

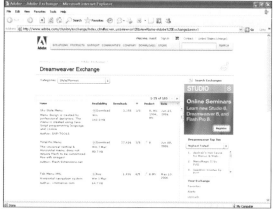

The Dreamweaver Exchange download site

In a nutshell, behaviors allow you to select interactive elements at the click of a mouse. Once activated and configured, the behaviors module writes the appropriate JavaScript for you. This code can be inspected and tweaked manually from Code view, but you don't actually have to write it yourself!

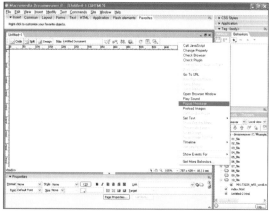

Easily adding a JavaScript in the Behaviors panel

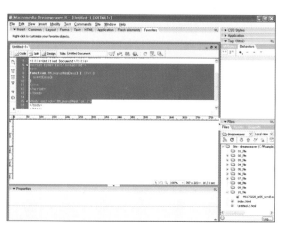

JavaScript as it appears in Code view

184

The Behaviors Panel

Let's explore the Behaviors panel. Select Window > Behaviors from the Menu bar. The Behaviors panel opens at the right of the Dreamweaver window.

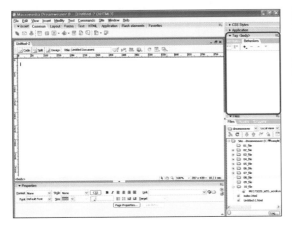
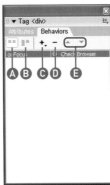

Ⓐ **Show set events**: Shows the list of defined events.

Ⓑ **Show all events**: All events are displayed in the list.

Ⓒ **Add behaviors**: A new behavior is added.

Ⓓ **Remove behaviors**: Existing behaviors are removed.

Ⓔ **Action order buttons**: You can change the order of actions.

Events and Actions

To insert interactive content using JavaScript, you need to understand events and actions. An "event" refers to the user's behavior, while an "action" is a response to the user's behavior. For example, if a user clicks linked text to go to a linked site, clicking the linked text is an event and going to the linked site is an action.

Click linked text with mouse	Event
Go to linked site	Action

To produce a highly interactive Web page, you need to use a variety of events. However, not all events are available on all Web browsers. Generally speaking, the more up-to-date a user's browser, the more events it will support. When you're applying behaviors to your site designs, you'll need to decide how "modern" you want your site to be. Just be aware that the more advanced your events are, the more likely it is the site won't work for all your visitors.

In Dreamweaver, you can configure the behaviors selection to reflect different HTML standards. This feature will help you choose appropriate events for the browsers you think your users will be using.

❶ Start Dreamweaver and select File > New from the Menu bar to open a new work window. (If there is no work window open in Dreamweaver, you cannot activate the Behaviors panel.)

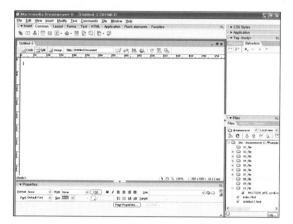

❷ Select Window > Behaviors from the Menu bar to activate the Behaviors panel. Then click the ⊞ icon in the Behaviors panel.

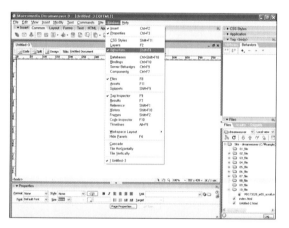

❸ A pull-down menu appears. Move your mouse pointer to Show Events For to bring up the submenu shown here.

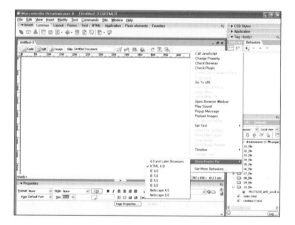

186

❹ Click HTML 4.01 from the submenu. Selecting this means that you will use only those events that can be used in version 4.01 or higher of the HTML standard. One of the main reasons for choosing HTML 4.01 is that it offers a variety of behavior-specific events. There are different types of events that may or may not be usable, depending on the viewer's Web browser. However, HTML 4.01 shows the list of events that can be used by all Web browsers, so you can more conveniently select events for a specific behavior.

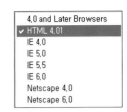

❺ Click Show all events in the Behaviors panel to see the list of available events. Note that more events are available in newer browser versions. There are many behavior events but not all of them are used. The most frequently used among them are those that can be used in HTML 4.01.

Standard Events

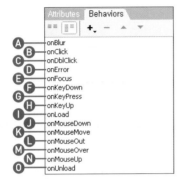

Ⓐ **onBlur**: Triggers an action when the mouse pointer is taken away from an item with a designated event.

Ⓑ **onClick**: Triggers an action when the object is clicked once with the left mouse button.

Ⓒ **onDblclick**: Triggers an action when the object is double-clicked with the left mouse button.

Ⓓ **onError**: Triggers an action when there is an error following the click of an element or link.

Ⓔ **onFocus**: Triggers an action when the mouse pointer is brought to an item with a designated event.

Ⓕ **onKeyDown**: Triggers an action when a key on the keyboard is pressed down.

Ⓖ **onKeyPress**: Triggers an action when a key on the keyboard is released after being pressed.

Ⓗ **onKeyUp**: Triggers an action when a key on the keyboard is not pressed.

Ⓘ **onLoad**: Triggers an action when the Web browser reads a specified element (image, text, etc.) in a page.

Ⓙ **onMouseDown**: Triggers an action as long as an object is clicked and held.

Ⓚ **onMouseMove**: Triggers an action when the mouse moves within a specified range.

Ⓛ **onMouseOut**: Triggers an action when the mouse moves away from the area specified by onMouseOver.

Ⓜ **onMouseOver**: Triggers an action when the mouse is over an element linked by the <a> tag.

Ⓝ **onMouseUp**: Triggers an action when the mouse is released after an onClick or onMouseDown event.

Ⓞ **onUpload**: Triggers an action when the current page changes to another page or is closed.

Basic Actions

The standard actions available in Dreamweaver are described below. Many additional actions can be downloaded from various Web sites.

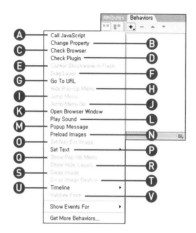

ⓐ Call JavaScript: Allows users to directly apply scripts.

ⓑ Change Property: Changes a property of a selected object.

ⓒ Check Browser: Checks the version of a user's browser and shows the events available for that version.

ⓓ Check Plugin: Checks which plug-ins are available in the user's browser.

ⓔ Control Shockwave or Flash: Controls Shockwave or Flash animations.

ⓕ Drag Layer: Allows a user to freely move the layer in a Web browser.

ⓖ Go to URL: Goes to a Web page when an event occurs.

ⓗ Hide Pop-Up Menu: Hides a pop-up menu.

ⓘ Jump Menu: Controls many links in a list/menu format.

ⓙ Jump Menu Go: While Jump Menu immediately goes to the linked page, Jump Menu Go performs that action when the Go button is clicked.

ⓚ Open Browser Window: Opens a new browser window. You can control elements of the window, such as title bar, menu bar, and scroll bar.

ⓛ Play Sound: Plays sound.

ⓜ Popup Message: Displays a message in a warning dialog box.

ⓝ Preload Images: Displays cached images from previous site visits. (When a viewer visits the site for the first time, static images are stored in their temp folder. On subsequent visits, these stored images are displayed rather than newly downloaded files.)

ⓞ Set Nav Bar Image: Uses images to create a navigation bar.

P **Set Text**: Enables you to choose a format for showing text.

Q **Show Pop-Up Menu**: Shows a pop-up menu.

R **Show-Hide Layers**: Controls which layers are displayed in the Web browser.

S **Swap Image**: Swaps an image in response to an event.

T **Swap Image Restore**: Replaces a swapped image with the original image.

U **Timeline**: Allows you to play, stop, or move to a specific frame in an animation that was created using the Timeline panel.

V **Validate Form**: Verifies the integrity of information that is entered in a form. For example, the Validate Form action can be used to ensure that users don't select user names that are already in use when they register on a Web site.

Creating a Simple Behavior

In this section, we will learn how to add a pop-up message to a Web page using behaviors.

1 Open a new work window. It is recommended that you save the document as soon as you open a new window.

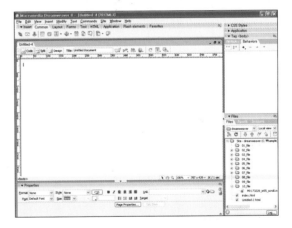

2 Click the ⊞ icon in the Behaviors panel and select Popup Message.

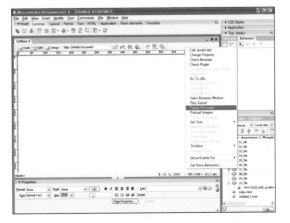

❸ When the Popup Message dialog box opens, as shown in the figure, enter "Dreamweaver 8" and click the Next button.

❹ You can see that the Popup Message action has been set in the Behaviors panel. If the onLoad event is not showing, you should select onLoad.

❺ Click the Split button to see Code view and Design view at the same time. Check the inserted code in Code view.

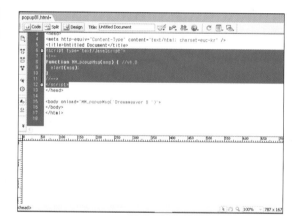

❻ Save the edited document and press F12 to preview it in a Web browser. When the Web browser opens, the message "Dreamweaver 8" appears in a warning dialog box.

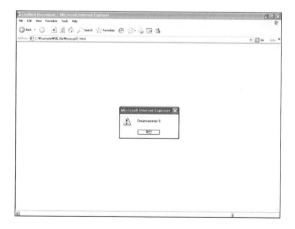

Using the Open Browser Window Behavior

The Open Browser Window behavior is often used to create pop-up windows that display important announcements for a Web site. In this exercise, we'll create an Open Browser Window action controlled by the onLoad event, so that a new window will open as soon as users load the primary Web page.

Source File
\Sample\08_file\open.htm

Start File
\Sample\08_file\open_new.htm

Final Files
\Sample\08_file\open_end.htm,
\Sample\08_file\open_new_end.htm

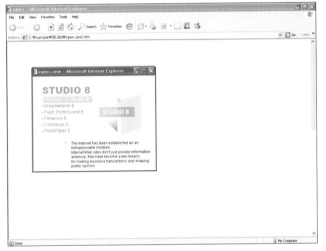

Final page

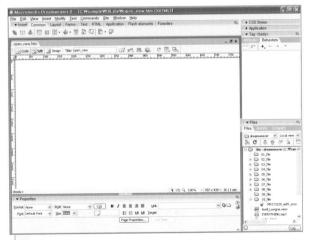

1 Select File > Open from the Menu bar to open the file \Sample\08_file\open_new.htm. You can get the same result by dragging the file from the Files panel (on the right) to the work window.

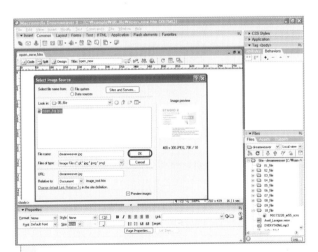

2 Select Common > Image from the Insert bar to insert the image \Sample\08_file\ open_bg.jpg into the document.

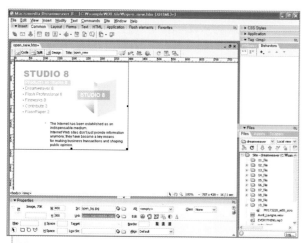

3 | Select the inserted image and set the link to "http://www.macromedia.com/" in the Properties inspector.

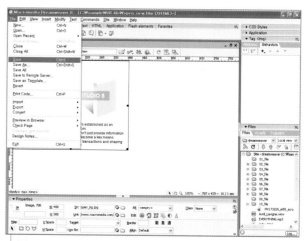

4 | Select File > Save from the Menu bar to save the edited document, then close the open_new.htm file.

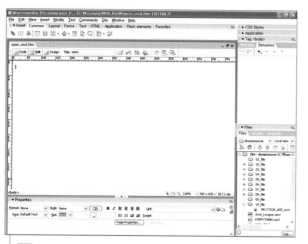

5 | Select File > Open from the Menu bar to open the file \Sample\08_file\open.htm.

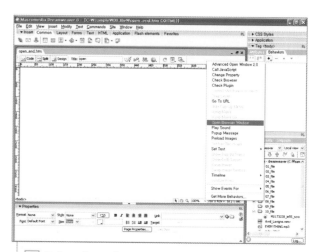

6 | Select Open Browser Window from the Behaviors panel.

7 | When the Open Browser Window dialog box appears, enter the values shown below.

note >>>

Settings for Step 7

URL to display: open_new.htm
Window width: 400
Window height: 300

tip >>

Open Browser Window is a default behavior of Dreamweaver. It opens a new browser window in response to an event.

Ⓐ **URL to display**: Select a file to load when the Open Browser Window action is activated.

Ⓑ **Window width**: Determines the width of the new browser window.

Ⓒ **Window height**: Determines the height of the new browser window.

Ⓓ **Attributes**: Allows you to show or hide each element of the browser, such as menu bar, scroll bar, and so on.

Ⓔ **Window name**: Allows you to assign a window name to the newly opened window.

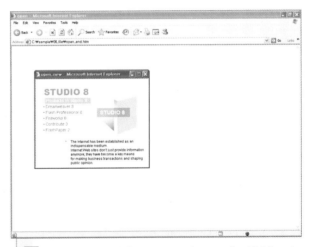

8 Check in the Behaviors panel to see whether the event for Open Browser Window is set to onLoad.

9 Save the edited document and press the F12 key to preview it. A new browser window opens, and the preset image appears. Open Browser Window is frequently used to show advertisements and announcements to visitors.

Open Browser Window doesn't let you determine the position of the browser window, but the Advanced Open Window behavior does. However, Advanced Open Window is not a default embedded behavior in Dreamweaver: you can download the Advanced Open Window extension from the Adobe Dreamweaver Exchange site. (Installing and activating extensions will be covered later in this book.)

As shown in this figure, Advanced Open Window enables you to set the relative position of a browser window under Dimensions by choosing a button to the right of Window, Position, and On Screen.

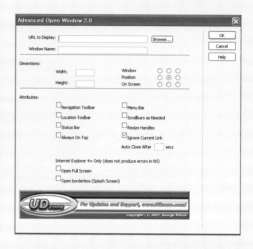

Fixing Spacing Problems with Open Browser Window

Image files (such as *.jpg files) and HTML documents can be loaded using the Open Browser Window feature. However, new windows are opened using the default settings of the viewer's Web browser, which leave space on the top and left sides of the window. As a result, the image or HTML document will seem pushed to the bottom right of the window.

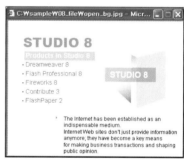

Open Browser Window, without the spacing adjustment

With this in mind, it is recommended that you set the dimensions of the new window larger than the source image or HMTL document to lessen the effect.

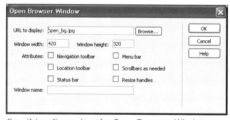

Specifying dimensions for Open Browser Window

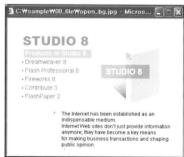

The same window, with the spacing adjustment

Creating a Navigation Menu Using Swap Image

It's common on the Web to see navigation menus that react to mouse events. This is typically handled using rollover commands in JavaScript. In Dreamweaver, the Swap Image behavior tackles the coding so you don't have to. In this exercise we'll show you how it's done.

Start File

\Sample\08_file\swapimage.htm

Final File

\Sample\08_file\swapimage_end.
htm

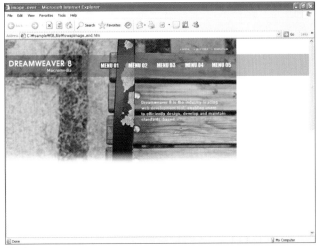

Final page

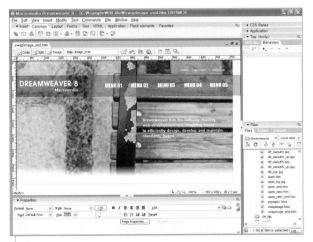

1 Open the file \Sample\08_file \swapimage.htm. This is the same file we used in the earlier exercise involving rollover images.

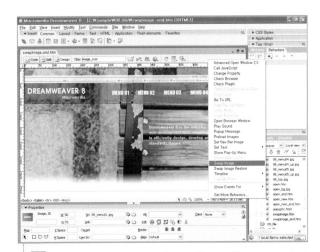

2 When inserting images for a rollover effect, you select and insert both a regular image and an "over" image. With Swap Image, you insert the regular image first and then apply the over image. Click the MENU 01 image and then select Swap Image from the Behaviors panel.

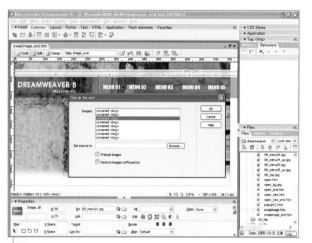

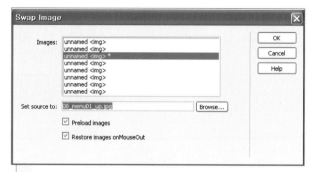

3 The Swap Image dialog box appears. You should be cautious here. If you have not assigned a name to the selected image, several "unnamed <img>" filenames appear in the Swap Image dialog box, with one among them already selected. You should not select another name. If you need to differentiate between these files, you should name each of the images in the Properties inspector.

4 In the Swap Image dialog box, click the Browse button for Set source to and select "08_menu01_up.jpg." Then click the OK button.

tip >>

Naming Images

Generally, when inserting images into a Document window, you don't give individual names to those images. There is no problem associated with not assigning names to each image, and often there are so many images that it would be difficult to name them all. However, to apply a behavior that uses these images, the images involved will need to have names. Note that if the "unnamed <img>" file that is selected by default is accidentally deselected, you will not be able to find the image again without a great deal of trial and error. In this case, you should probably remove the behavior and reapply it to save time.

5 As shown in the figure, onMouseOut: Swap Image Restore and onMouseOver: Swap Image have now been added to the Behaviors panel.

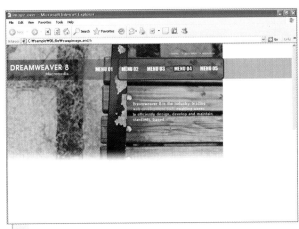

6 Save the edited document and press the F12 key to preview it. When you move your mouse pointer to the MENU 01 image, the over image now appears, as shown in the figure.

7 Apply Swap Image in the same way to the other menu images.

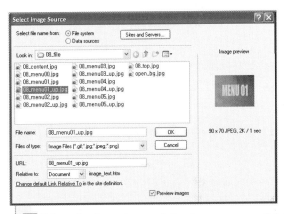

8 You can change the over image for any of the links from the Behaviors panel. Click the MENU 05 image and then select onMouseOver: Swap Image from the Behaviors panel.

9 When the Swap Image dialog box appears, click the Browse button for Set source to and select another file. Here we will choose 08_menu01_up.jpg (the same image we selected for MENU 01).

10 Save the edited document and press the F12 key to preview it. When you move your mouse pointer to the MENU 05 image, the new over image appears, as shown in the figure.

This is what the JavaScript and source code created by Swap Image look like. The code for all the menu images would take up too much space, so only the code for one menu image is shown. Needless to say, behaviors save an incredible amount of time compared to coding by hand.

● **JavaScript**

```
<script type="text/JavaScript">
<!
function MM_preloadImages() { //v3.0
  var d=document; if(d.images){ if(!d.MM_p) d.MM_p=new Array();
    var i,j=d.MM_p.length,a=MM_preloadImages.arguments; for(i=0; i<a.length; i++)
    if (a[i].indexOf("#")!=0){ d.MM_p[j]=new Image; d.MM_p[j++].src=a[i];}}
}

function MM_swapImgRestore() { //v3.0
  var i,x,a=document.MM_sr; for(i=0;a&&i<a.length&&(x=a[i])&&x.oSrc;i++) x.src=x.oSrc;
}

function MM_findObj(n, d) { //v4.01
  var p,i,x;  if(!d) d=document; if((p=n.indexOf("?"))>0&&parent.frames.length) {
    d=parent.frames[n.substring(p+1)].document; n=n.substring(0,p);}
  if(!(x=d[n])&&d.all) x=d.all[n]; for (i=0;!x&&i<d.forms.length;i++) x=d.forms[i][n];
  for(i=0;!x&&d.layers&&i<d.layers.length;i++) x=MM_findObj(n,d.layers[i].document);
  if(!x && d.getElementById) x=d.getElementById(n); return x;
}

function MM_swapImage() { //v3.0
  var i,j=0,x,a=MM_swapImage.arguments; document.MM_sr=new Array; for(i=0;i<(a.length  2);i+=3)
    if ((x=MM_findObj(a[i]))!=null){document.MM_sr[j++]=x; if(!x.oSrc) x.oSrc=x.src;
x.src=a[i+2];}
}
//    >
</script>
```

● **Source Code**

```
<table width="100%" border="0" cellspacing="0" cellpadding="0">
  <tr>
    <td width="295"><img src="08_menu00.jpg" width="295" height="70" /></td>
      <td  width="90"><img  src="08_menu01.jpg"  width="90"  height="70"  id="Image1"
onmouseover="MM_swapImage('Image1','','08_menu01_up.jpg',1)" onmouseout="MM_swapImgRestore()"
/></td>
    <td width="95"><img src="08_menu02.jpg" width="95" height="70" /></td>
    <td width="95"><img src="08_menu03.jpg" width="95" height="70" /></td>
    <td width="90"><img src="08_menu04.jpg" width="90" height="70" /></td>
    <td width="95"><img src="08_menu05.jpg" width="95" height="70" /></td>
    <td bgcolor="#CFA980"> </td>
  </tr>
</table>
```

Creating Submenus Using Show-Hide Layers

Show-Hide Layers is a behavior used to control layers. In this exercise, we will control submenus using the Show-Hide Layers behavior.

Source Files
\Sample\08\08_show_sub01.png,
08_show_sub02.png,
08_show_sub03.png,
08_show_sub04.png

Start File
\Sample\08_file\showlayer.htm

Final File
\Sample\08_file\showlayer_end.htm

Final page

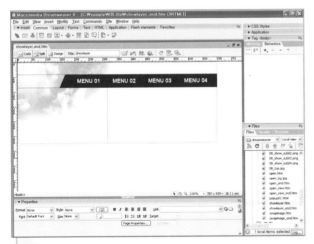

1 Select File > Open from the Menu bar to open the file \Sample\08_file\showlayer. htm.

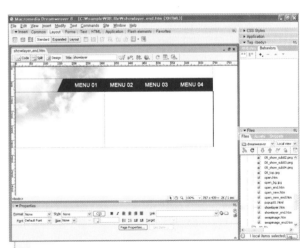

2 Select Layout from the Insert bar.

199

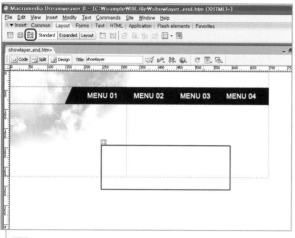

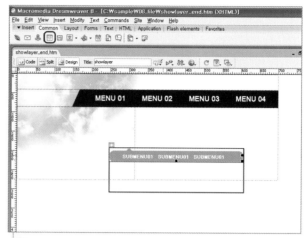

3 Now select Draw Layer from the Insert bar. Create a layer as shown by dragging the mouse.

4 With the layer selected, select Common > Images from the Insert bar to insert the following image into the layer: \Sample\08_file\08_ show_sub01.png.

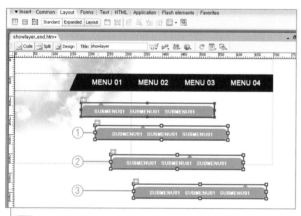

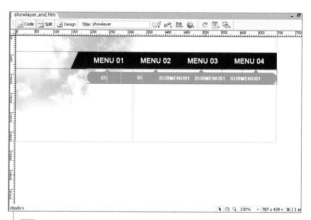

5 In the same manner, insert images for the other three submenus.

6 Place all the layers under the main menu as shown in the figure.

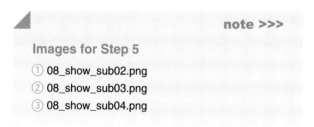

note >>>

Images for Step 5

① 08_show_sub02.png
② 08_show_sub03.png
③ 08_show_sub04.png

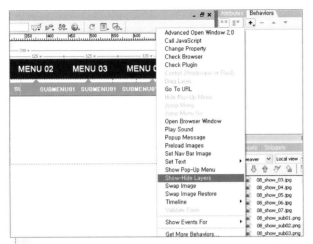

7 Select the MENU 01 image and then select Show-Hide Layers from the Behaviors panel.

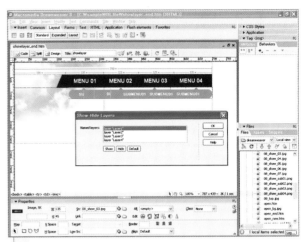

8 Enter the text shown below in the Show-Hide Layers dialog box and click the OK button. (Show Layer1 and hide the other layers.)

```
layer "Layer1" (show)
layer "Layer2" (hide)

layer "Layer3" (hide)
layer "Layer4" (hide)
```

tip >>

Show-Hide Layers

The Show-Hide Layers action shows or hides layers in response to an event. Select the name of the layer; click the Show button to show it or the Hide button to hide it. Even if you don't assign names to layers, they are automatically named "Layer1," "Layer2," and so on. You can apply actions to layers using these names.

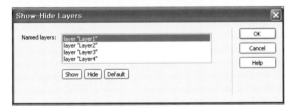

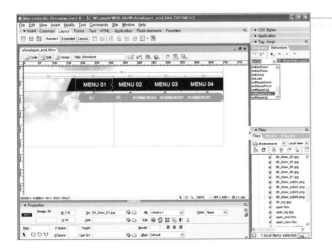

9 You can see that the Show-Hide Layers action has been added to the Behaviors panel. Make sure that the event is set to onMouseOver. If not, change it to onMouseOver.

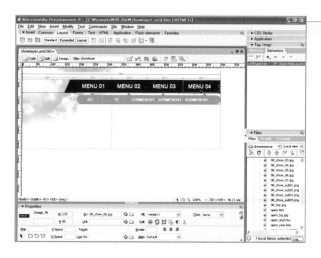

10 In the same manner, apply Show-Hide Layers for the other menu images according to the table below.

MENU 02	MENU 03	MENU 04
layer "Layer 1"(hide)	layer "Layer 1"(hide)	layer "Layer 1"(hide)
layer "Layer 2"(show)	layer "Layer 2"(hide)	layer "Layer 2"(hide)
layer "Layer 3"(hide)	layer "Layer 3"(show)	layer "Layer 3"(hide)
layer "Layer 4"(hide)	layer "Layer 4"(hide)	layer "Layer 4"(show)

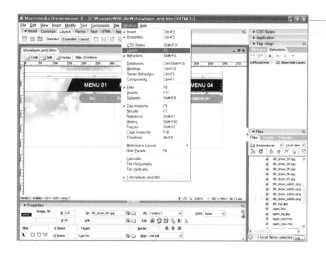

11 When the Show-Hide Layers settings are finished, select Window > Layers from the Menu bar to open the Layers panel.

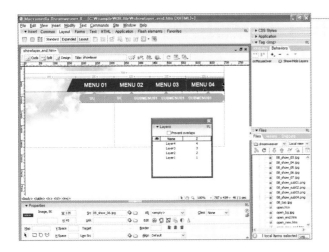

12 Click the eye-shaped icon until the closed-eye icon is shown for all layers. These settings will hide all layers so they can't be seen when the browser window first opens.

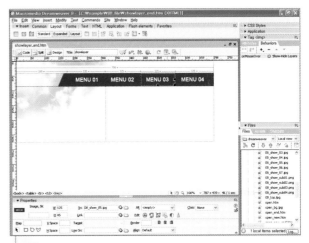

13 Save the edited document and press the F12 key to preview it. When you move the mouse cursor to each main menu image, its submenu appears.

14 To change the settings for Show-Hide Layers, first select the image you wish to change in the Document window. In this case, select MENU 03.

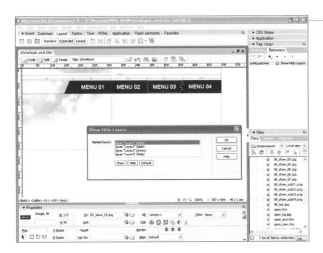

15 When you select the image, the Behaviors panel is activated and you can change the settings if you double-click the Show-Hide Layers action.

Exploring Extensions for Infinite Expansion of Behaviors

To supplement the behaviors included with Dreamweaver, you can download additional behaviors—called extensions—from Adobe's Web site. Some behaviors are free, but others must be purchased. This section describes the process of adding an extension. We will learn more about extensions in Chapter 10.

01 Click the + button in the Behaviors panel and then select Get More Behaviors. Alternatively, you can select Help > Dreamweaver Exchange from the Menu bar.

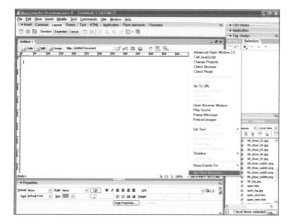

02 As shown in the figure, the Adobe Web site opens to a page where you can review the list of behaviors that can be added.

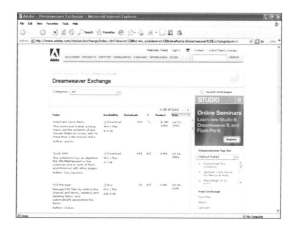

03 The Adobe Web site offers some free behaviors and sells others. You can select and download behaviors and install them in Dreamweaver.

04 To install the extensions for a downloaded behavior, start the Macromedia Extension Manager. Macromedia Extension Manager is automatically installed when you install Dreamweaver. In Microsoft Windows, click Start > All Programs > Macromedia > Macromedia Extension Manager, or double click on the downloaded extension file to start it.

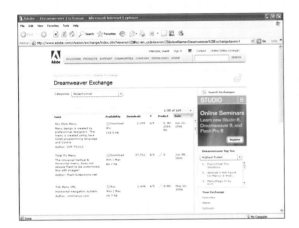

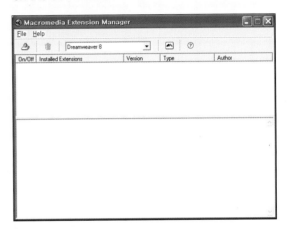

05 When Macromedia Extension Manager is started, click the Install New Extension icon, or select File > Install Extension from the menu bar.

06 When the Select Extension to Install dialog box appears, select the downloaded extension file and click the OK button. When the License Agreement dialog appears, click the Accept button.

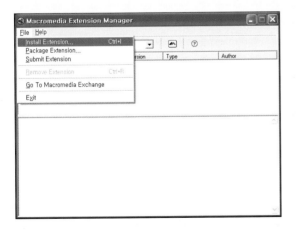

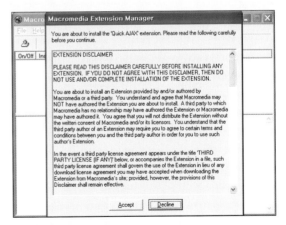

07 When the installation is completed, a message appears to inform you that the installation of the extension is finished. To use the extension properly, you must restart Dreamweaver.

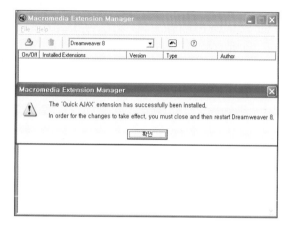

08 New extensions are shown in the Macromedia Extension Manager.

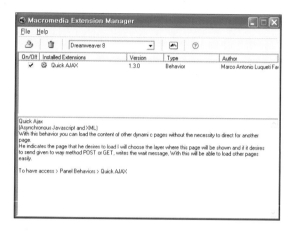

09 After restarting Dreamweaver, added extensions are available in the Behaviors panel.

10 If you want to temporarily stop using installed extensions, disable them by toggling the On/Off checkbox for the extensions in Macromedia Extension Manager. If you use Macromedia Extension Manager to disable an extension while Dreamweaver is open, you must restart Dreamweaver.

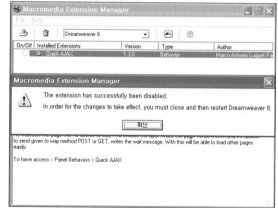

11 If you want to completely remove installed extensions, select the extensions in Macromedia Extension Manager and click the Remove Extension (🗑) icon. When a dialog box appears to confirm the deletion of the extensions, click Yes.

12 You can see that the deleted extensions have been removed from the list in Macromedia Extension Manager.

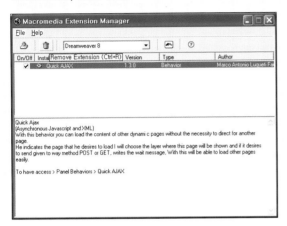

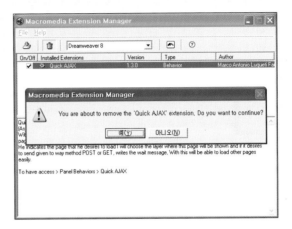

Chapter 9

Inserting Multimedia Content

In Dreamweaver, you can insert and control multimedia content such as video, audio, and Flash movies as easily as you would normal content. We'll learn how in this chapter, and then explore what multimedia content can do for your pages through a series of exercises.

Multimedia on the Web

As you might expect, Dreamweaver allows you to add multimedia content to your pages without having to dig around in HTML. In this section we'll cover the basics for working with video, audio, and Flash content.

Video Formats

Since video files tend to be relatively large, distributing them on the Web can be tricky. As a result, streaming technology is typically used for real-time playback, and video files are usually compressed to the point of image degradation. Fortunately, this is typical enough on the Web that users have grown accustomed to the limitations of Web video.

There are two main formats for Web video: Microsoft's WMV and Apple's MOV.

Windows Media Player inserted into a Web document

WMV (Windows Media Video), created by Microsoft, is one of the most widely used video formats on the Web. It offers excellent video quality at reduced file sizes, which often allows site designers to place WMV videos at larger sizes. Another strength of the WMV format is that it provides excellent support for streaming; site visitors can view WMV videos as they download. WMV videos also support digital rights management (DRM), so videos can be encoded to prevent duplication and distribution.

Windows Media Player

WMV files are played by Windows Media Player by default. Since this player is included by default when Windows is installed, the WMV format is a safe bet when building sites, because you can be fairly certain that most site visitors have the software required to view these files.

Apple's QuickTime format is another widely used format on the Web, thanks to Apple's superb technology. It supports all the high-end features provided by Microsoft's WMV format—excellent compression ratios, widespread compatibility, DRM, streaming, etc. The choice between QuickTime and WMV often comes down to preference, but there are a couple of things to consider with QuickTime. On the potentially negative side, the QuickTime player is third-party software for Windows users, so you can't assume that all site visitors will be able to view QuickTime videos by default. On the positive side, Apple's iPod prefers Apple's video format, so videos encoded in their format have the potential for iPod-based distribution. Ultimately, your choice between formats will likely come down to personal preference and your site's intended audience.

Apple QuickTime

You can insert video files in Dreamweaver by clicking Common > Plugin from the Insert bar. A Select File window will open from which you can select the desired video file to be inserted into your page.

Sound Formats

Audio on the Web can be divided into two categories: music and sound effects. The specific purpose you have in mind will often dictate the audio format you go with.

- **∗.mid**: The MIDI (Musical Instrument Digital Interface) format is exclusively for instrumental music. Because MIDI files trigger sounds hosted on the user's computer (via a MIDI-compatible sound card), their file sizes are very small, which makes them well suited to the Web. However, the sound quality is inconsistent and often undesirable.

- **∗.wav**: The WAV (Waveform Extension) format is used to deliver high-quality sound. Because WAV files are not compressed (and therefore tend to be quite large), they are seldom used in Web sites. They are sometimes used for short sound effects, though, since the format is so widely supported by Web browsers and sound editing software.

- **∗.mp3**: The MP3 (MPEG Audio) format is the most popular digital format. This format achieves small file sizes through high compression rates. The degree of compression depends on the compression method used, but typically one minute of sound translates to around 1 MB of data. MP3 files can be played in a wide variety of programs.

There are a number of ways to insert sound files using Dreamweaver. For example, you can insert sound by using the HTML tag for background sound: <bgsound>.

```
<bgsound src="Path of music file">
```

However, background sound supports a limited number of sound formats and cannot be controlled by the user. The <bgsound> tag has the following characteristics:

- You don't need to set display options because no media player is displayed.
- Only *.wav files can be played.
- Load time is long because the entire file must be downloaded before it can be played.

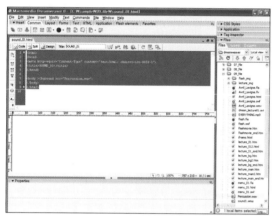

```
<html>
<head>
<meta http equiv="Content    Type"
content="text/html; charset=iso    8859
1">
<title>SOUND_01</title>
</head>

<body >
<bgsound src="Percussion.wav">
</body>
</html>
```

\Sample\09_file\sound_01.html

By contrast, the <embed> tag allows users to control playback, and audio can be streamed. Sound played by the <embed> tag uses the default media player in the user's operating system.

```
<embed src="music URL">
```

The <embed> tag has the following characteristics:

- Most streaming formats can be played.
- Files can be played while loading via streaming.
- Various options can be used to customize playback, such as Autostart, Display Hidden, Width and Height, Loop, Volume, etc.

In Dreamweaver, select Common > Plugin from the Insert bar and click a file you wish to insert.

```
<html>
<head>
<meta http  equiv="Content   Type" content="text/html; charset=iso   8859   1">
<title>SOUND_02</title>
</head>

<body>
<embed src="EVERYTHING.mp3" width="400" height="400"></embed>
</body>
</html>
```

212

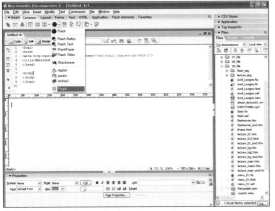

Selecting a plug-in type for inserting media

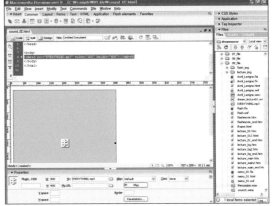

Code view of a media file inserted into a document

The <embed> tag options are shown below.

```
<embed src="music file" width="400" height="400" type="audio/x  pn  realaudio  plugin"
controls="controlpanel" autostart="false" volume="1" ></embed>
```

After selecting an inserted movie file, click on the Parameter button in the Properties inspector. You can then set options for the embedded file; add options by clicking on the [+] button.

- **Autostart**: Choose whether or not to start music automatically ("true": music starts upon loading; "false": music does not start upon loading).

- **Hidden**: Choose whether or not to display the user's media player ("true": player is shown; "false": player is hidden).

- **Width and Height**: Use to adjust the player size.

- **Loop**: Use the Loop option to determine whether the audio file plays repeatedly. Entering "true" or "-1" will loop the audio infinitely. If you enter "false," or "1," the audio will be played only once. Entering another number will play the audio a matching number of times.

- **Volume**: Set the desired volume by inputting a number between 0 and 100.

Flash Files

Flash is the most widely used multimedia format on the Web at present. Embedded Flash movies can bring animation, sound, video, and even interactivity to Web sites. As a result, the format is extremely popular as a method for making sites more dynamic and visually stimulating.

There are two file formats associated with Flash: .fla and .swf. FLA is the source file format used by Adobe's Macromedia Flash program; this is the native program used to create Flash content. Flash movies created in Flash (the program) are saved in the SWF format, which is what Web designers embed in their pages for distribution to site visitors. SWF files are not editable.

213

Note that, although you can insert Flash files and even create basic Flash elements within Dreamweaver, you cannot edit *.fla files from within the program. To do this you must use Adobe's dedicated Flash software.

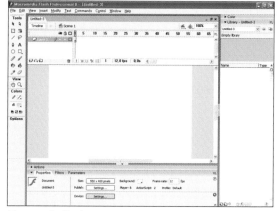

Macromedia Flash

Creating a Flash Button within Dreamweaver

You can insert Flash files from the Insert bar just as with images and tables.

❶ Start Dreamweaver and select File > New from the Menu bar to open a new work window.

❷ Select Common > Flash Text from the Insert bar.

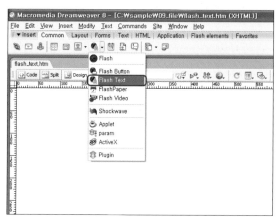

❸ When the Insert Flash Text dialog box opens, enter the values shown here and click the OK button to insert them.

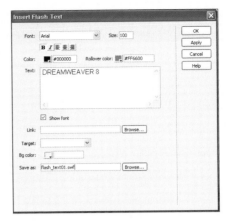

note >>>

Settings for Step 3

Font: Arial
Size: 100
Color: #000000
Rollover color: #FF6600
Text: DREAMWEAVER 8
Save As: flash_text01.swf

❹ You can see that the Flash content has been inserted.

❺ Select File > Save from the Menu bar to save the edited document. Press the F12 key to preview it. The Flash content that has been inserted changes text color when you move your mouse over it.

note >>>

For instructions detailing how to insert SWF files (created in the Macromedia Flash program) in Dreamweaver, see Exercise 2 of this chapter, Inserting a Flash Video.

Exploring Multimedia Formats

This table lists some of the most common multimedia formats found on the Web.

ASF	Streaming video format from Microsoft
ASX	Format for linking multiple video files
AVI	Video file format for Windows; uncompressed
MID	Sound file format that triggers audio samples stored on the user's computer
MP3	Sound file format with excellent compression
MOV	Video file format for Macintosh, now also supported on Windows
MPEG	Video file format with good compression
RA	Real-time audio transfer file format by Real Audio
RM	Real-time image transfer file format by Real Audio
RAM	Real-time video transfer file format by Real Audio
SWF	The standard format used for Flash files
VIV	Video file format that can achieve high video quality with excellent streaming and compression
WAV	Sound file format; uncompressed
WMA	Sound file format (streaming) that has a higher compression rate than MP3 without loss of sound quality
WMV	The standard video format for Microsoft Windows; supports high file-size compression without degrading sound and image quality

Inserting Video Using the Embed Tag

The most frequently used tag for inserting multimedia content in HTML is the <embed> tag. In this exercise, we will insert a video using the <embed> tag to create a multimedia home page.

Source Files
\Sample\09\lecture_bgimg.jpg, dream_lecture01.avi

Start Files
\Sample\09_file\lecture_main.htm, lecture_bg.htm, lecture_01.htm

Final Files
\Sample\09_file\lecture_main_end.htm, lecture_bg_end.htm, lecture_01_end.htm

Final page

1 Open the example file \Sample\09_ file\lecture_bg. htm.

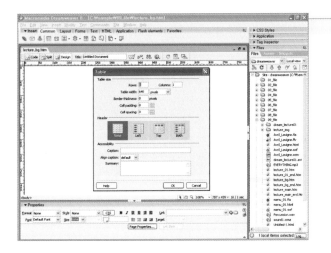

2 To insert a table, select Common > Table from the Insert bar. When the Table dialog box appears, enter the values shown below and click the OK button.

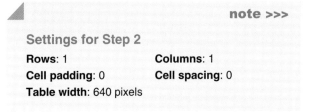

note >>>

Settings for Step 2

Rows: 1   **Columns**: 1

Cell padding: 0   **Cell spacing**: 0

Table width: 640 pixels

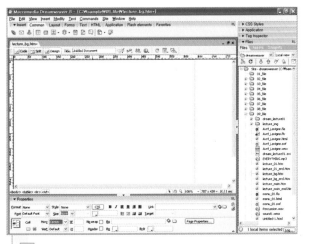

3 Set the table height to 520 pixels and choose Center for the cell alignment setting.

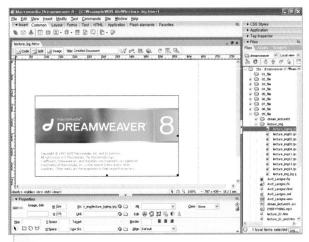

4 Move the mouse cursor into the cell and choose Common > Images from the Insert bar to insert the image lecture_bgimg.jpg (found in the folder lecture_img). Select File > Save As from the Menu bar to save the edited document as \Sample\09_file\lecture _bg2.htm and close the file.

5 Open the file \Sample\09_file\lecture_01.htm in Dreamweaver.

218

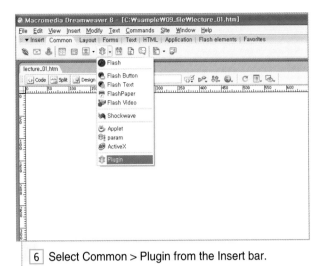

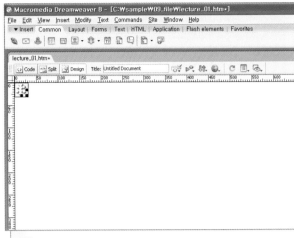

| 6 | Select Common > Plugin from the Insert bar. |

| 7 | When the Select File dialog box appears, select the file \Sample\09_file\dream_lecture01.avi. Then click the OK button. |

tip >>

Inserting the Embed Tag

There are many methods for inserting the <embed> tag in an HTML document. You can type it in manually when in Code view or insert it by clicking Common > Plugin from the Insert bar.

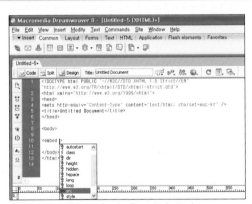

Directly inputting the ⟨embed⟩ tag in Code view

If you use icons in the Insert bar to insert the <embed> tag, the <object> tag will also be inserted. However, if you use Common > Plugin, only the <embed> tag will be inserted. Note that you must use the <embed> tag when working with most forms of multimedia content.

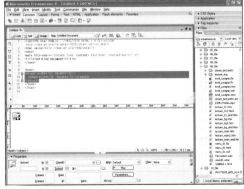

The ⟨embed⟩ tag, along with the ⟨object⟩ tag

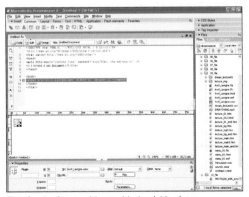

The ⟨embed⟩ tag, without with the ⟨object⟩ tag

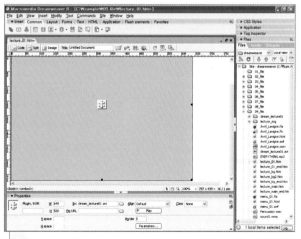

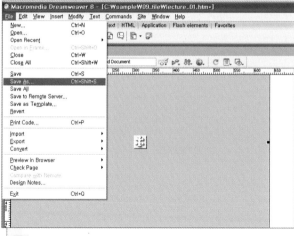

8 Select the inserted video content and set the values shown below in the Properties inspector.

9 Select File > Save As from the Menu bar to save the edited document as \Sample\09_file\lecture_012.htm and close the file.

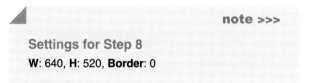
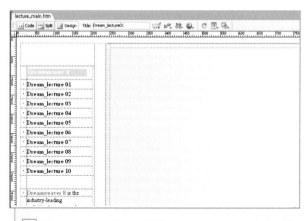

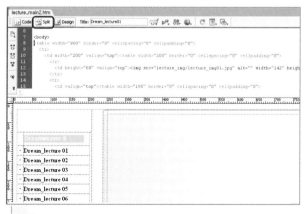

10 The preparation of files is now complete. To continue, open /Sample/09_file/lecture_main.htm.

11 Click the Split button to see Code view and Design view at the same time.

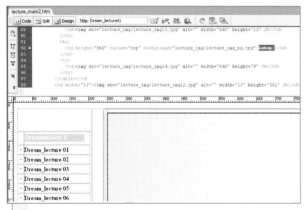

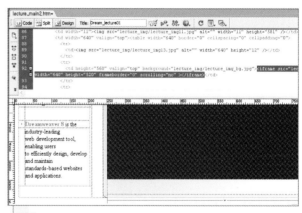

12 When you move the mouse cursor into the wide cell in Design view, the mouse cursor in Code view also moves to the selected cell.

13 Insert the code shown between <td> and </td> in the selected cell. Because we specified the name "lecture," set the link target to "lecture."

```
<iframe src="lecture_bg2.htm" name="lecture"
width="640" height="520" frameborder="0"
scrolling="no" ></iframe>
```

tip >>

iframe

The <iframe> tag is used to insert an HTML document into another HTML document. The advantage of <iframe> over the <frame> tag is that you can specify the dimensions and location of the inserted HTML document. However, be aware that scroll bars will appear if the size of the inserted HTML document is larger than the designated area.

```
<html>
<head>
<meta http equiv="Content  Type" content="text/html; charset=iso  8859  1">
<title>Untitled Document</title>
</head>
<body>
<table width="900" border="0" cellspacing="0" cellpadding="0">
  <tr>
     <td><iframe src="http://www.yahoo.com" name="aaa" width="450" height="250" frameborder="0"
></iframe></td>
    <td> </td>
  </tr>
  <tr>
    <td> </td>
     <td><iframe src="http://www.hp.com" name="sss" width="450" height="250" frameborder="0"
></iframe></td>
  </tr>
</table>
</body>
</html>
```

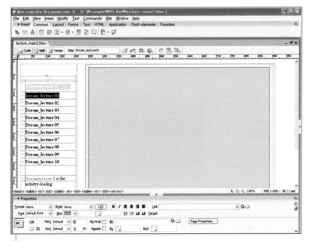

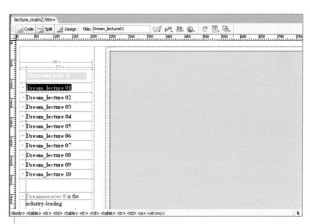

14 Click the Design button to display only Design view. Then select the text "Dream_lecture 01" as a block from the left side of the window.

15 To link the selected text, enter the values shown below in the Properties inspector.

note >>>

Settings for Step 15

Link: lecture_012.html, **Target**: lecture

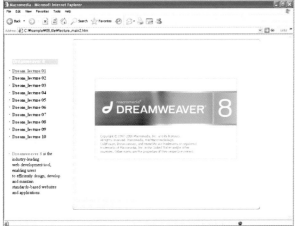

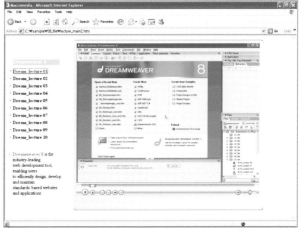

16 Save the edited document and press the F12 key to preview it. The two HTML documents appear at the same time, as shown here.

17 Click Dream_lecture 01 in the left menu. A video lecture starts to play in the window.

Exercise

2

Inserting a Flash Video

Flash content is the most widely used multimedia format on the Web. Popular uses include animated ads and site intros. It's even possible to create entire Web pages purely in Flash. In this exercise, we'll insert a Flash video into a Web page.

Final page

Source File
\Sample\09_file\flash.swf

Start File
\Sample\09_file\flashmovie.htm

Final File
\Sample\09_file\flashmovie_end.htm

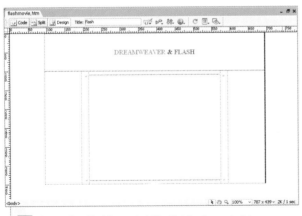

1 Open the file \Sample \09_file\flashmovie.htm.

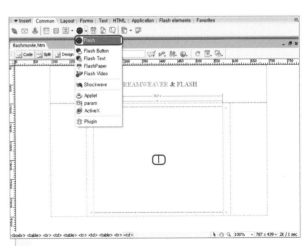

2 Move the mouse pointer into the middle cell and click Common > Flash on the Insert bar.

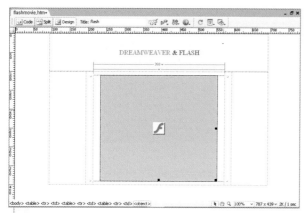

3 When the Select File dialog box appears, select the file \Sample\09_file\flash.swf. Then click the OK button to check the Flash file.

4 Save the edited document and press the F12 key to preview it. The Flash video plays.

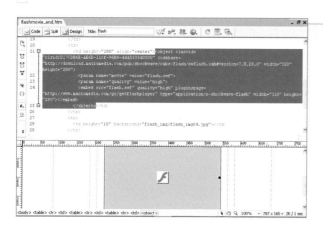

5 You can check the source code for the inserted Flash file. Click the Split button to see Code view and Design view at the same time.

```
<object    classid="clsid:D27CDB6E    AE6D    11cf    96B8    444553540000"
codebase="http://download.macromedia.com/pub/shockwave/cabs/flash/swflash.cab#version=7,0,19,0"
width="320" height="280">
        <param name="movie" value="flash.swf">
        <param name="quality" value="high">
                                <embed    src="flash.swf"    quality="high"
pluginspage="http://www.macromedia.com/go/getflashplayer" type="application/x    shockwave    flash"
width="320" height="280"></embed>
        </object>
```

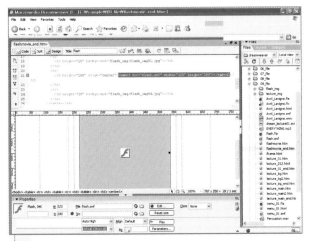

6 You can see that the Flash video has been inserted using the <object> and <embed> tags. However, you can play a Flash video with a simple <embed> tag, as shown below.

```
<embed    src="flash.swf"    width="320"
height="280"></embed>
```

Chapter | 10

Advanced Techniques

To close out the book we'll cover a grab bag of Dreamweaver's more advanced features, including extensions, the Assets panel, templates, and libraries. These features allow you to expand Dreamweaver's functionality while increasing your effeciency and productivity.

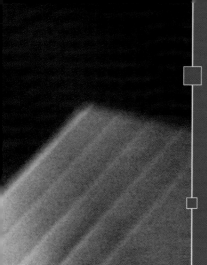

Going Pro

Developing professional techniques will dramatically improve your efficiency and the quality and complexity of your Web sites. In this section we'll introduce some key concepts to expand your Dreamweaver horizons.

Types of Extensions

Extensions are plug-ins that add new features to Dreamweaver. You can download an impressive variety of extensions from the Adobe Exchange Web site (http://www.adobe.com/cfusion/exchange) and install them using Macromedia Extension Manager. (Alternatively, you can simply double-click a downloaded extension file.) After installing an extension, restart Dreamweaver and check for its addition under the Insert tab, in the Commands menu, or in the Behaviors panel, depending on the type of extension.

Object Extensions

Object extensions refer to features that can be added to the Insert bar. These extensions allow the insertion of image or multimedia file types that were not previously supported in Dreamweaver.

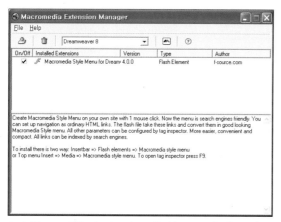

Installing an Object extension with Macromedia Extension Manager

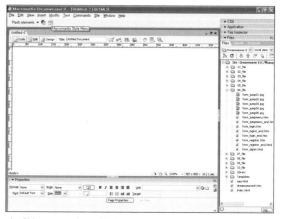

An Object extension added to the Dreamweaver Insert bar

Command Extensions

Command extensions refer to features that can be added to the Commands menu. Some examples are Live Clock, which allows you to insert a clock in a specific area; Resize Window, which allows you to control the size of a window with just a click of a mouse; and Scrollbars, which allows you to insert iframes and colored scrollbars.

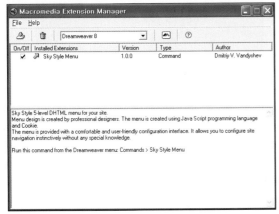

Installing a Command extension with Macromedia Extension Manager

A Command extension added to the Dreamweaver Command menu

Behavior Extensions

Behavior extensions are added to the Behavior panel when installed. A variety of extensions are available from various sources on the Web (including Adobe's site), each of which adds functionality beyond Dreamweaver's default behaviors. Open Browser Window and Advanced Open Window are good examples.

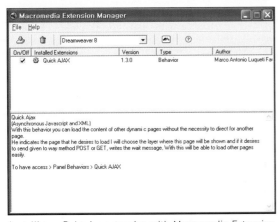

Installing a Behavior extension with Macromedia Extension Manager

A Behavior extension added to the Dreamweaver Behaviors panel

The Assets panel allows you to easily organize and manage a large volume of images, tables, text, Flash elements, and other content. It achieves this by letting you add source files to your pages simply by dragging and dropping them from the panel, rather than opening them one-by-one through the File > Open method.

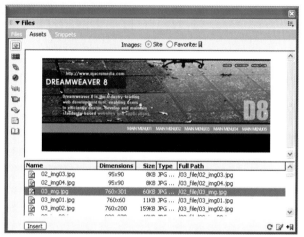

The Assets panel

The Assets panel is located in the Files panel group. There are nine asset types provided, and these assets are all in the local root folder defined by the site. (For the most part, the Assets panel catalogs all the assets contained in the currently opened site.)

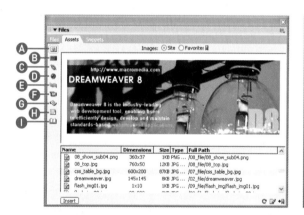
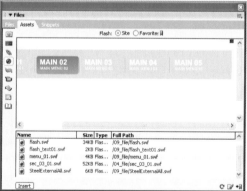

Ⓐ Images: Shows the image files that are in GIF, JPEG, and PNG formats. The current paths are displayed, so you can review the exact locations of images.

Ⓑ Colors: Shows the colors of text, background, and links used in both the documents and style sheets of the site.

Ⓒ URLs: Shows the external links of the current site. Link types in this category include FTP, GOPHER, HTTP, HTTPS, JavaScript, E-mail (MAILTO), and local file (FILE://).

Ⓓ Flash: Shows Macromedia Flash files. The Assets panel shows only the output SWF files, not the FLA (Flash source) files.

Ⓔ Shockwave: Shows Macromedia Shockwave files. The output files created by Macromedia's Director are displayed.

230

F **Movies**: Shows QuickTime or MPEG files.

G **Scripts**: Shows JavaScript or VBScript files. However, those scripts that are included in HTML files but are not independent JavaScript or VBScript files are not displayed in the Assets panel.

H **Templates**: Templates are used to apply the same page layout to multiple pages. Editing a template allows you to conveniently change the layout of all pages that use the template.

I **Library**: Library items are specific elements that are used in multiple pages. When a library item is changed, all pages that contain that library item are updated.

Managing Content with Libraries

When creating pages for a Web site, you may use similar tables, images, and text repeatedly. If you save these repeated elements in a library, you can use them more conveniently.

1 Click the Assets panel in the Files panel group. Then click Library and New Library Item.

2 Save the new library icon as "600_table."

231

❸ Click the Edit icon. The 600_table.lbi file opens, as shown here.

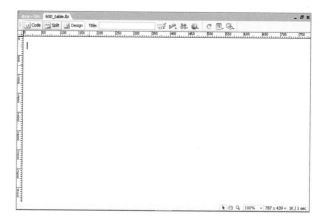

❹ Insert a table into the 600_table.lbi file. Give the table a width of 600 and save the file.

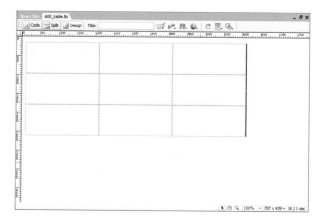

❺ Create a new HTML document and drag-and-drop the 600_table.lbi file into the work window. The library file is inserted into the new document, as shown here. After inserting a library file into multiple pages like this, you can simply edit the library file to update all pages that contain that library file.

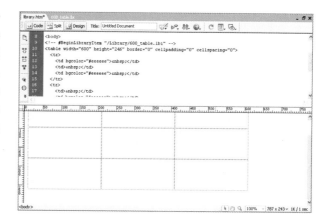

tip >>

In general, libraries included in HTML documents cannot be edited within those HTML documents. However, you can delete library properties from the inserted library object to convert it to general HTML tags. To do this, select a desired library item and click the Detach from original button.

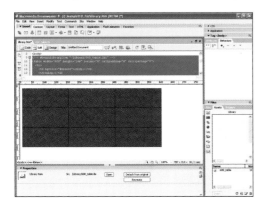 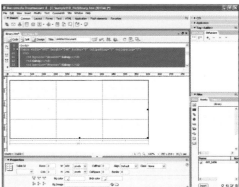

1

Downloading, Installing, and Using Extensions

The number of extensions that can be added to Dreamweaver is virtually infinite. You can install and use as many extensions as your computer capacity allows. You can download free extensions and those for sale from the Adobe Web site.

Final page

Downloading Extensions

We will now download a free extension from the Adobe Web site. Before downloading, you should first apply for an Adobe membership account.

1 Web developers are constantly creating new extensions, which are provided by Adobe through its Web site. Access the Adobe site (http://www.adobe.com/) and click the Your Account button.

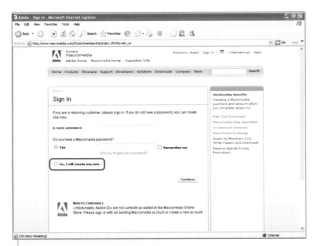

2 If you are a registered member, enter your e-mail and password. Otherwise, check the "No, I will create one now" button to apply for a new account.

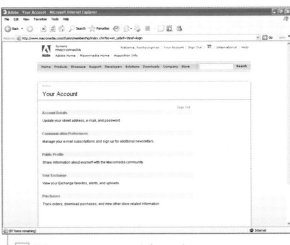

3 When your account information appears, you are logged in.

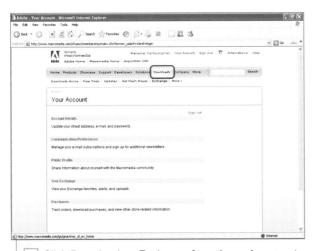

4 Click Downloads > Exchange from the main menu to access the Macromedia Exchange page.

5 There are two ways to find desired extensions. When you wish to browse or don't know the exact name of an extension, you can look at all the extensions one-by-one. To do this, select All (below Dreamweaver Exchange) and click More.

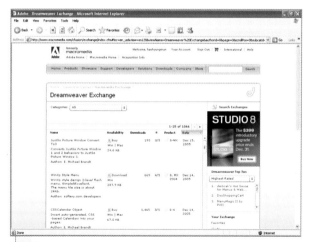

6 All the available Dreamweaver extensions are displayed with simple descriptions.

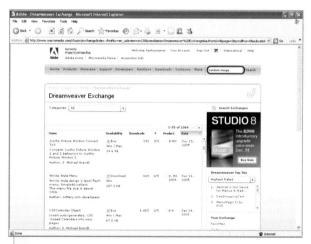

7 The second method is to use the search feature in the upper-right corner of the Web site. For example, type "random image" in the search keyword input box and then run the search.

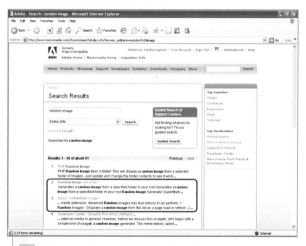

8 The search results for "random image" are displayed as shown here. Click "Advanced Random Images" from the search results.

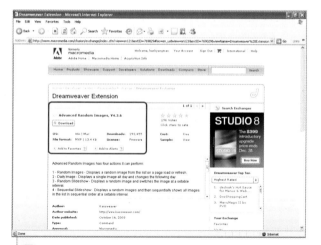

9 On the details page for the Advanced Random Images extension, click the Download button to download that extension.

[10] As mentioned previously, there are free extensions and those you must pay for. Fortunately, the Advanced Random Images extension is in the former category. You might be surprised by some of the useful additions you can make to Dreamweaver's functionality without getting out your credit card.

Installing Extensions

Once you download an extension, it must be installed. This is done through the Macromedia Extension Manager (generated when Dreamweaver is installed). Now we will install the extension we just downloaded.

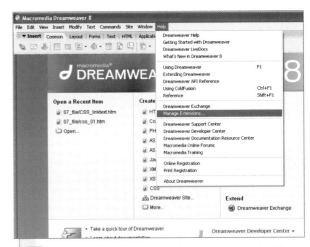

[1] Select Help > Manage Extensions from the Menu bar.

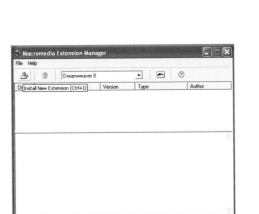

[2] When the Macromedia Extension Manager dialog box appears, click the Install New Extension icon.

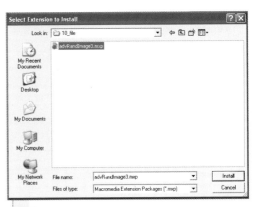

[3] Select the advRandImage3.mxp file that you downloaded and click the Install button.

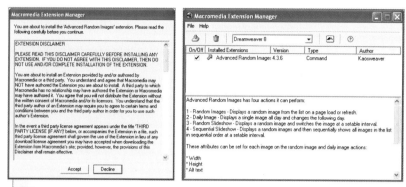

4 When the install dialog box appears, click the Accept button to install the new extension. In the Macromedia Extension Manager dialog box, you can now see the Advanced Random Images extension.

5 You can see the new menu item inserted into Dreamweaver, as shown in the figure.

tip >>

The Adobe site also provides extensions for Fireworks and Flash.

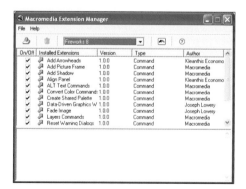

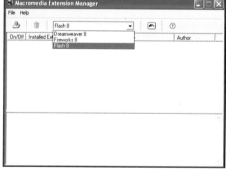

Using Extensions

We will now apply the Advanced Random Images extension to a page in Dreamweaver. This particular extension presents various images, one by one, within a specified space, and at random time intervals.

Start File
○ \Sample\10_file\advRandImage.htm

Final File
○ \Sample\10_file\advRandImage_end.htm

Final page

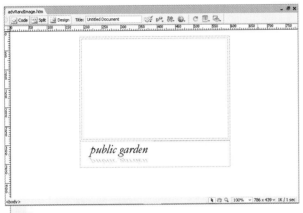

☐1 Open the file \Sample\10_file\ advRandImage.htm.

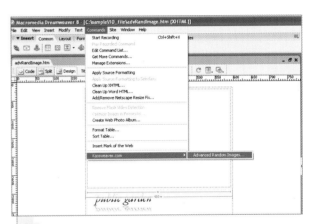

☐2 Place your mouse cursor in the large cell and select Command > Kaosweaver.com > Advanced Random Images from the Menu bar, as shown in the figure.

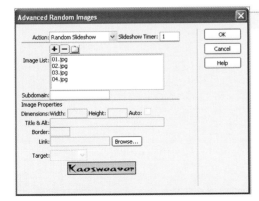

☐3 When the Advanced Random Images dialog box appears, set the values shown here and click the OK button.

note >>>

Settings for Step 3
Action: Random Slideshow
Slideshow Timer: 1
Image List: 01.jpg, 02.jpg, 03.jpg, 04.jpg

4 The first random image is now displayed.

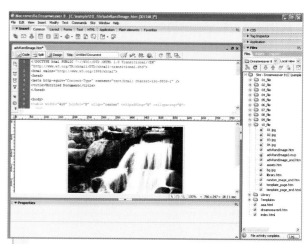

5 The image may appear, as shown above, or it may not. If the image does not appear, you should check the image path in Code view. Click the Split button to see Code view and Design view at the same time.

```
// Advanced Random Images Start
// Copyright 2001-2002 All rights reserved, by
Paul Davis - www.kaosweaver.com
   var j,d="",l="",m="",p="",q="",z="",KW_ARI=
new Array()
// KW_rs[1000]
  KW_ARI[KW_ARI.length]='/10_file/01.jpg';
  KW_ARI[KW_ARI.length]='/10_file/02.jpg';
  KW_ARI[KW_ARI.length]='/10_file/03.jpg';
  KW_ARI[KW_ARI.length]='/10_file/04.jpg';
  j=parseInt(Math.random()*KW_ARI.length);
  j=(isNaN(j))?0:j;
                        document.write("<img
name='randomSlideShow' src='"+KW_ARI[j]+"'>");
function rndSlideShow(t,l) { // Random
Slideshow by Kaosweaver
   x=document.randomSlideShow; j=l; while
(l==j) {
       j=parseInt(Math.random()*KW_ARI.length);
j=(isNaN(j))?0:j; }
                        x.src=KW_ARI[j];
setTimeout("rndSlideShow("+t+","+j+")",t);
}
rndSlideShow(1000,0)
// Advanced Random Images End
```

6 Even though the images appear in Design view, there may be a problem with the image paths in Code view. Reviewing the code is a great way to troubleshoot.

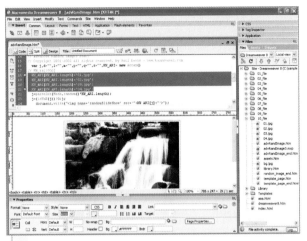

7 Change the image paths to relative paths, as shown below.

8 Save the edited document and press the F12 key to preview it. You can see that the images change every second.

```
// Advanced Random Images Start
// Copyright 2001-2002 All rights reserved,
by Paul Davis - www.kaosweaver.com
  var j,d="",l="",m="",p="",q="",z="",KW_ARI=
new Array()
// KW_rs[1000]
  KW_ARI[KW_ARI.length]='01.jpg';
  KW_ARI[KW_ARI.length]='02.jpg';
  KW_ARI[KW_ARI.length]='03.jpg';
  KW_ARI[KW_ARI.length]='04.jpg';
  j=parseInt(Math.random()*KW_ARI.length);
  j=(isNaN(j))?0:j;
                    document.write("<img
n a m e = ' r a n d o m S l i d e S h o w '
src='"+KW_ARI[j]+"'>");
function rndSlideShow(t,l) { // Random
Slideshow by Kaosweaver
  x=document.randomSlideShow; j=l; while
(l==j) {
      j=parseInt(Math.random()*KW_ARI.length);
j=(isNaN(j))?0:j; }
                    x.src=KW_ARI[j];
setTimeout("rndSlideShow("+t+","+j+")",t);
}
rndSlideShow(1000,0)
// Advanced Random Images End
```

2

Creating and Editing a Template

Saving and modifying templates is quite simple in Dreamweaver. In this exercise we'll walk you through the basic procedure for a table-based page layout.

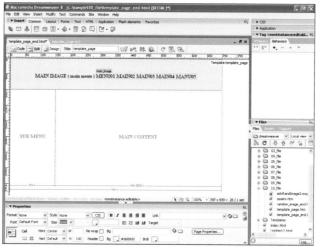

Final page

Start File
\Sample\10_file\template_page.htm

Final File
\Sample\10_file\template_page _end.htm

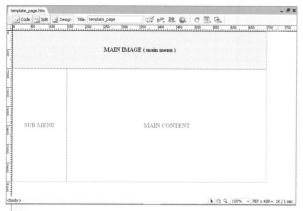

1 Open the file \Sample\ 10_file\template_page.htm.

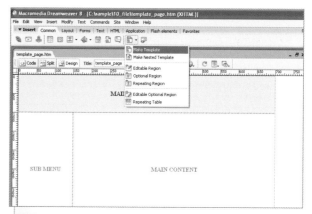

2 Select Common > Templates > Make Template from the Insert bar.

3 In the Save As Template dialog box, enter "template_page" in Save as. Click the Save button.

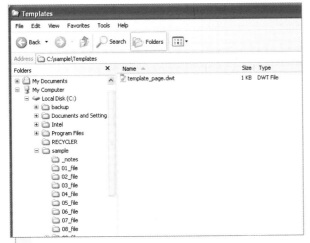

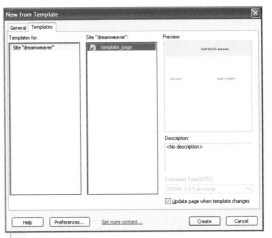

4 In Windows Explorer, you can see that the file Templates\template_page.dwt has been created in the sample folder.

5 Close all work windows and select File > New from the Menu bar to load the template_page.dwt. Select the template_page.dwt file in the Templates tab of the New from Template dialog box. Then click the Create button.

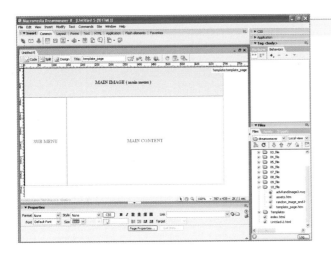

6 As shown in the figure, the stored template appears. The template filename is also displayed at the top-right corner of the work window. Save the file as \Sample\ 10_file\template_page_end.htm.

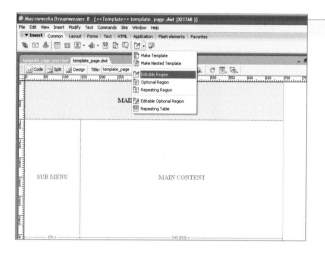

7 Move the mouse cursor over the text "MAIN IMAGE" and select Common > Templates > Editable Region from the Insert bar.

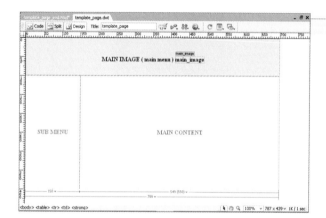

8 Enter "main_image" for Name in the New Editable Region dialog box and click the OK button. The "MAIN IMAGE" cell is now set as an editable region, as shown in the figure. Editable regions allow you to update numerous pages (using the same template) with a single edit.

tip >>

Template Updates

Once you make a template, it can still be changed. When you edit a *.dwt file, Dreamweaver asks you whether you want to automatically apply the edited content to all files that are based on that template. Simply click Update to modify all the corresponding pages.

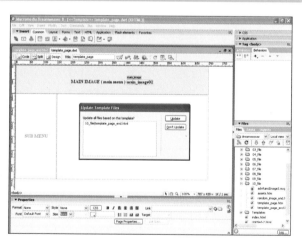

Index > > >